The Saco DRIVE-IN

Cinema Under the Maine Sky

CAMILLE M. SMALLEY

THE History PRESS

Published by The History Press
Charleston, SC 29403
www.historypress.net

First published 2014

Manufactured in the United States

ISBN 978.1.62619.453.3

Library of Congress CIP data applied for.

To the Saco Drive-In's most-loved owner, Eugene V. Boragine, and his wife, Helen Toth; to his vision; and to all of the carloads of movie fans, both past and present, who enjoy the magic of the Saco Drive-In.

CONTENTS

ACKNOWLEDGEMENTS

I would like to thank everyone who contributed memories for this book and all of the Saco Drive-In patrons, from opening day in July 1939 to the families who watch movies there today. Without your continuing support, love of film and enjoyment of the drive-in theater, the Saco Drive-In could not have existed for seventy-five years. I think Eugene and Helen would be proud that the theater in which they invested so much time is still running today and is very successful.

I would also like to thank my good friend and talented photographer Charlie Widdis of Charlie Widdis Photography for taking beautiful photos of the Saco Drive-In and helping make my artistic vision come true. I knew I wanted artistic, modern photographs of the Saco Drive-In, so I turned to the best photographer I know. Charlie, I could not be more grateful to you.

To Mandy Wertman, thank you for listening to me talk through various historical timelines and theories, suggesting several horror film history books to me and often allowing me to think out loud, sometimes not making coherent sense when I had another "But what about this?" idea.

Bryan McLeod, you've been such a helpful support to me, from asking me how writing is going to reminding me of my strengths and offering to assist in any capacity. You are such an amazing, loving person, and your support means the world to me. I don't know what I would do without it, and I love you.

Thank you to Michael Strout of Michael Strout Photography for the beautiful author photo and to Brigid McGovern for all the good coaching and support.

ACKNOWLEDGEMENTS

Ashley Brooks, thanks for reading one of the earliest drafts of the e-book; it's always helpful to get perspective from a fellow writer!

Ry Russell, thank you for asking me to help with this project in its infancy, and I look forward to continuing to work with you into the Saco Drive-In's seventy-fifth anniversary in 2014.

Justin Chenette, I don't know what else to say to you. You and I have been powering through projects together like superheroes, and I don't know what I would do without you. Thank you for initially collecting the memories for this book and for working with me on the first few steps; it could not have happened without you and our many working afternoons at various locations.

I would like to thank Renee DesRoberts, Jeff Cabral and the staff of the McArthur Library for all their help while I used their microfilm machines and for allowing me to use images from their collections in this book. It's fantastic to have such a great working relationship with another Maine archival institution, and I had such a great time researching in their archive.

Brittany Vara, thanks for all your support and love from the first day I told you about the first project to writing this book.

To Tara Raiselis and Leslie Rounds at the Dyer Library and Saco Museum, thank you for always supporting my projects and offering your editing services. Also, thank you to Jill Jakeman, a whiz with genealogy.

Thanks to my parents and grandparents for all their support, especially my grandmother, who carried an article from the *Portland Press Herald* in her purse for weeks.

Jennifer Tuttle, thank you for your editing help and inspiration. I couldn't have made it through the last two drafts without you.

And last but not least, thank you to Elizabeth A. DeWolfe for all of your continuing support, assistance, assurance, shoulder for tears and so much more. You've always been a role model, mentor, colleague and friend to me—words cannot express my gratitude!

Feature 1

A HISTORY OF THE SACO DRIVE-IN

The Saco Drive-In Opens

Movies, popcorn, the laughter of children and the buzz of mosquitoes—what could be better on a warm summer evening? Maine's first drive-in theater opened in 1939 with a screening of *Forbidden Music*, starring Jimmy Durante and June Clyde, accompanied by a Disney cartoon and a newsreel that probably contained scenes from the developing war in Europe.[1]

The Saco Drive-In is located on a stretch of road between Saco and Scarborough commonly called Route 1 or the Portland Road. This historic roadway has existed since the eighteenth century, when the English citizens who immigrated to the area constructed the highway as a route to Scarborough.[2] The Portland Road gained more traffic in the mid-nineteenth century as transportation technology changed and railroads brought more people to the area, meaning more stagecoaches traveled to and from Saco. By the 1870s, tourists from as far away as New York sought refuge and entertainments at the beaches in Saco, Biddeford and Old Orchard Beach. As automobiles traversed Route 1 in the 1920s, cabins like Cascades Inn, motels and restaurants like Angellmere dotted the landscape, frequently offering the quintessential Maine shore dinner. Ticket booth attendants at the Saco Drive-In often gave out programs during the summer to keep patrons informed about the happenings and places to visit along Route 1.

SACO

Open Air Theatre

Route No. 1
Portland Road
SACO

-:- PROGRAM -:-
WEEK OF AUG. 28, 1949

YOUR MODERN THEATRE
R.C.A. SPEAKER
IN EVERY CAR

Above: "Pre-Show." *Photograph by Charlie Widdis Photography©.*

Left: A 1949 Saco Drive-In program. *Courtesy of James Leary.*

With the influx of cars and vacationers, the Saco Drive-In had the perfect location to draw in eager film fans both "from away" and local.

Cinema quickly became a mainstay amusement in American culture, and the earliest film fans attended movies in quiet, indoor theaters. These theaters, typically owned by Hollywood companies like MGM, RKO and Paramount, had rules of etiquette and propriety for patrons.[3] Film fans in Saco could attend theaters in Portland or later, in 1927, at their own indoor Mutual Theater, located at 268 Main Street in downtown Saco. While indoor theaters boasted air conditioning, the inside of the automobile at the local drive-in offered a more relaxed social environment.[4] Surrounded by trees and located at the edge of town, the drive-in offered a private yet public place to enjoy films. While the theater was often filled with laughing children and families, the inside of one's own automobile allowed for space and comfort, as well as a sense of privacy within the cab.

After World War II, automobile fever gripped America. The car gave families the freedom to drive anywhere—including places like the drive-in for leisure—and maintain the same level of comfort found in one's own home. The car meant families could travel away from the physical home space but still experience time together at places like the drive-in theater. The large vehicles of the late 1940s and '50s gave drive-in patrons plenty of room to enjoy "the talkies" in the comfort of their own cars. Early advertisements drew attention to "the talkies" and emphasized the family atmosphere by offering cartoons. Whereas early films were silent, often accompanied by just music to set the mood for the film, by the 1930s, commercialized films with sound were the mainstay. For example, 1936's *Modern Times* was the first time anyone heard Charlie Chaplin's voice on the big screen.

The Saco Drive-In was the first outdoor movie theater of its kind in the state of Maine and the second in New England. By the 1950s, the popularity of the drive-in had exploded, and owners built theaters from coast to coast. Moviegoers often referred to drive-ins by several different names, including the term "ozoner," which referred to the outdoor experience of the drive-in. Others preferred "passion pit," as the darkness and privacy of the drive-in theater allowed many teenage romances to blossom within the confines of the car.[5] This classic, all-American amusement has undergone a variety of changes in its eighty-one-year history, both as an entertainment experience and as a physical space, including the addition of concession stands and playgrounds, upgrades to the sound systems, film deals with major Hollywood production companies, new digital technology and so much more.

The Motor-In Theatre on Route 1 in Saco celebrates a second season, featuring newsreels in addition to a double feature. From the May 1940 *Biddeford Daily Journal. McArthur Public Library Archives, Biddeford, Maine.*

The popularity of the drive-in theater began to decline in the 1960s, and many drive-ins closed throughout the 1970s and '80s.[6] As cities and suburban towns like Saco expanded, the land drive-ins occupied became more and more valuable, and developers made theater owners generous offers for their property. Indoor theaters with two or three screens transformed into giant multiplexes with stadium-style seating, offering multiple screens and film selections for movie patrons. The small, single-screen drive-in theater could not compete with this multiplex expansion. In the twenty-first century, many people can enjoy films with the click of a button or a tap on the screen and stream content over the Internet without even having to leave their living rooms or bedrooms. Young people, more independent than in previous generations, have new activities and demands to fill their time. Yet despite new entertainment options, the changing physical landscape and the activity-filled schedule of the twenty-first-century family, the Saco Drive-In has remained a cultural landmark and a family favorite.

A Brief History of Saco

Just as the Saco Drive-In and its patrons have experienced many changes throughout the ozoner's seventy-five-year history, the city of Saco and its citizens also have undergone many physical changes in terms of landscape, technology and economy since the early seventeenth century. Long before Samuel de Champlain visited the mouth of the Saco River in 1604, the Saco and other Abenaki natives called the land home.[7] The riverbanks provided a place for trade with the Malisleet, the Passamaquoddy and even the Micmac, who traveled from as far away as present-day Canada. These groups walked or used boats for their primary means of travel to the mouth of the Saco River.

Throughout the early seventeenth century, a variety of explorers traveled by ship to the Saco River and noted the tall trees, thick shrubbery and seemingly undeveloped land.[8] In 1616, English captain Richard Vines, sponsored by Sir Fernando Gorges of Plymouth Company, wintered in Saco Bay, located at the confluence of the Saco River and Atlantic Ocean.[9] After a successful winter, Vines returned throughout the decade and secured a patent to transport fifty people over the course of seven years (from 1630 through 1637) with the intention of establishing a settlement on the western bank of the river, currently known as Biddeford. On that same day, Captain

Richard Bonython and Thomas Lewis received the same patent for fifty emigrants to the eastern bank, known as Saco or Camp Ellis.[10]

Life during the first one hundred years at the Saco settlement was not easy. In these early years, the land known as Route 1 would have been nothing but tall trees and greenery. Farmers had difficulty clearing their land of thick shrubs and trees to make room for crops. Many found that it was easier to keep cows and pigs rather than struggle with the rigors of farming.[11] Saco Native Americans found themselves at odds with these new English immigrants, and disagreements often occurred. Despite the violence between the Native Americans and the New England colonists, the settlement managed to grow and developed a working economy. Using the tall trees that lined the river, shipbuilders constructed large sailing vessels for both coastal and international trade. Carpenters created clapboards that traveled to England in exchange for porcelain, cloth and other goods that were needed by the new settlement, and the bountiful seas provided cod for the developing fishing industry.[12] The diverse economy at the Saco River provided the baseline for a successful settlement.

By 1718, Saco had grown significantly.[13] As the population of the area increased, the center of town moved away from the mouth of the river and closer toward the falls near Indian Island, later Cutts Island (now Factory or Saco Island). William Pepperrell, a merchant from Portsmouth (later Sir William Pepperell), purchased a large tract of land on the east (Saco) side of the river. He sold tracts to various shipwrights and businessmen who developed lumber mills. The General Court of Commissioners for Massachusetts Bay decreed in 1718 that the residents of Wells, Biddeford, Buxton, Scarborough and Portland needed to create proper highways and roads, including a roadway to Portland.[14] Without the developed roadways, the Crown commissioners decided the Province of Maine could not officially hold court. At this time, citizens on the eastern bank laid out Main Street and Buxton, Portland and Ferry Roads.[15] Previously, most settlers had traveled via boat or by foot up the beach; however, the more formal roadways better suited the growing town. The Portland Road, known in the twentieth and twenty-first centuries as Route 1, became an official roadway between Saco and Portland.

With a higher population than before, residents on the east bank decided to construct their own meetinghouse due to the hardship of fording the Saco River repeatedly for services. In 1762, leaders petitioned the General Court of Massachusetts for the east bank to be its own district, separate from Biddeford.[16] With an influx of people settling in Saco, improvements to the road and travel systems became necessary. More roads through town were developed as more businesses moved into the area. Entrepreneur Colonel Thomas Cutts and his business partner, Josiah Calef, opened the first ironworks factory on Cutts Island. The ironworks supplied a variety of hardware to the shipbuilding industry, as well as for overseas trade. After Colonel Cutts's death, his son, Dominicus, sold the family land on Cutts Island to a consortium of Boston investors who brought the first brick-and-mortar textile factories to the area in the 1830s. In 1842, the railroad came to Saco, linking Portland, Saco, Portsmouth and Boston. With Saco on the rail line, more and more people came to work in the factories, started new businesses along Main Street or developed farms on rural North Saco land.[17] The Civil War in the 1860s slowed the textile production, which in turn affected the Saco economy. However, after the war, the Maine economy gained a new industry: tourism.

Taking a Walk on the Boardwalk

The Saco Drive-In would eventually benefit from and capitalize on the influx of summer visitors to the Saco Bay area. Initially, the sandy beaches provided a haven for the wealthy upper class and, much later, for church groups like the Salvation Army. In the 1780s, many upper-class individuals took time off to travel for their health. Elite members of American society traveled to hot springs or the seaside as a tonic to soothe the mind and the body.[18] Places like Saratoga Springs in New York flourished as popular health retreats designed to rejuvenate frazzled nerves and cure various ailments. After the Civil War in the 1860s, Old Orchard Beach became increasingly popular as a place of leisure and respite from urban living. In the 1870s, the modern "tourism" industry developed, and Old Orchard Beach attracted myriad people, from the wealthy to the lower classes, who sought a day of leisure by the shore.[19] By the 1930s, places like the Saco Drive-In, only a couple of miles from Old Orchard Beach, offered another type of leisurely amusement.

In 1840, Ebenezer C. Staples hosted the first foreign visitors at his boardinghouse in Old Orchard Beach.[20] His house was located a short distance from the Grand Trunk Railroad and the Portland, Saco and Portsmouth Railroad. These rail systems brought thousands of visitors from Canada and other points to Staples's front door by the mid-nineteenth century. By 1865, stagecoaches traveled frequently from Saco, Scarborough and Portland to Old Orchard Beach.[21] Clambakes on the beach enticed visitors, as did midnight excursions in the moonlight and picnics in a variety of picturesque locations. By the late nineteenth century, resorts and hotels began to appear on the formerly rural landscape and appealed primarily to visitors from New York and other heavily congested cities. Ocean Park and Old Orchard Beach offered a respite from the crowds, pollution and stresses of city life.

According to historian Roy Fairfield, the opening and completion of the Boston and Maine Railroad in 1873 was the single most significant event in the development of the Old Orchard Beach tourism industry.[22] This rail line intersected Saco's Main Street at the falls of the Saco River and continued to Old Orchard Beach, paralleling the beach and offering spectacular views of the Atlantic Ocean. With the steady increase of visitors, hotels continued to grow and specialize. Hoteliers designed their buildings specifically to provide high-end amenities that catered exclusively to the upper class, offering better views and first-class services and welcoming wealthy guests to a home away from home, separate from the day-trippers. The improvements in transportation systems, including more railroads, ferries and coaches, as well as the advancement of workers' rights and the advent of time off from work, meant vacations were available to the average worker.[23] More working-class people in the southern Maine area could afford to take brief, inexpensive vacations at Old Orchard Beach's less pricey establishments.

The seashore became a draw for many tourists and increased the amount of traffic through Saco to Old Orchard Beach. Church groups gathered at Saco's Ferry Beach, as well as at nearby Ocean Park, for outdoor retreats and worship. The Salvation Army and Universalists were among many groups who constructed outdoor amphitheaters for summer meetings. In 1881, the Maine Free Will Baptists built an octagonal temple at Ocean Park and held annual summer meetings there for the next three decades.[24] The Universalists held their annual camp meetings at Ferry Beach on Saco Bay, just a few miles from Ocean Park. The group met and established the Ferry Beach Association—still an active group at Ferry Beach today. Between church groups and the increasing numbers of tourists, Old Orchard Beach helped establish Maine as a "Florida" of the North, according to Roy Fairfield.[25] With such significant growth, it was not much longer until widespread use of automobiles in the early twentieth century would bring even more people to the area.

Driving to the Drive-In

In the 1880s, families spent leisure time taking the trolley to Old Orchard Beach, strolling around Pepperrell Park or perhaps enjoying a carriage ride or a bicycle journey. Automobiles, or "horseless carriages," came to Saco and Biddeford in 1900.[26] By 1930, there were 1,528 cars in the town of Saco, or 1 car for every five persons.[27] With the increase of auto traffic, more filling stations dotted the landscape, including along U.S. Route 1. More and more out-of-state license plates appeared on the roadways as automobiles became a widespread commodity, and many people found themselves spending their sunny summer days on the shores at Old Orchard, Ferry Beach or Biddeford Pool. Instead of taking a stroll by the large fountain in Pepperrell Park, families in 1939 preferred amusements like the Saco Drive-In.

Route 1, referred to as the "Highway of America" in a 1940 Saco Drive-In advertisement, was originally developed in 1820 as the Cumberland Turnpike and became the major route to Portland via Saco and Scarborough.[28] Between 1914 and 1934, the State of Maine spent $134 million on 1,427.86 miles of roadway.[29] In Saco, Route 1 has many names, including Elm Street, Main Street and, where the Saco Drive-In sits, the nearly three-hundred-year-old Portland Road. In 1925, Maine installed yellow and black numerical road signs, the earliest markers for a major highway in the United States.[30] As traffic along Route 1 increased, so did the businesses on this stretch of the road. Route 1 runs parallel to Ocean Park and Old Orchard Beach, connecting motorists to the beach, as well as inns, such as Cascades Inn and Angellmere, and other amusements like the Saco Drive-In.

While the Saco Drive-In was the first ozoner in Maine and is the United States' second-oldest drive-in still in operation, Camden, New Jersey, claims to be the birthplace of America's first drive-in. Richard Hollingshead Jr. opened the Park-In Theater on June 6, 1933, with *Wife Beware*, a 1932 film starring Adolphe Menjou. Hollingshead, son of Whiz Auto Products founder Richard Hollingshead Sr., invented the drive-in theater by placing a 1928 Kodak film projector on the hood of his car. He tested the projection at various angles and in varying weather conditions, ultimately creating a theater of cars in a staggered pattern parked in front of a large outdoor screen. Hollingshead applied for and received a patent for the drive-in on May 16, 1933.[31] The Park-In Theater permitted the Loews Theater to use the drive-in concept for a nominal royalty fee, which allowed Loews to expand from being exclusively an indoor theater. As other states, even as far

From the September 2, 1939 *Biddeford Daily Journal. McArthur Library Archives, Biddeford.*

away as California, began to create drive-in theaters, many new owners did not credit Hollingshead or pay royalties.

New England's first ozoner, the Weymouth Drive-In, opened in 1936 in Weymouth, Massachusetts. In 1948, drive-in development ranged from $75,000 to $100,000 for the basic drive-in, plus a minimum of another $20,000 in amenities such as a playground or a picnic area.[32] Later, in 1950, the judicial system invalidated the drive-in patent, and any enterprising businessperson could use the concept.[33] In 1946, only 102 drive-in theaters existed in the United States; however, in 1949, that increased by nearly ten times to 1,000.[34] As the country's economy improved after World War II, drive-ins sprang up from coast to coast across the United States.

In the 1950s, the birthrate in the United States skyrocketed. In the postwar economy, women married at younger ages than their mothers had in the pre-drive-in era and settled into homes with their husbands to start families.[35] The United States government sanctioned this familial resurgence by passing the Housing Act of 1949, which gave contractors incentives to build single-family homes in the growing suburban landscape. The Federal Housing Authority assisted with this by passing zoning laws to create new neighborhoods, playgrounds and schools and to serve other community needs. Veteran mortgage loans enabled many former soldiers to obtain home loans on houses in the suburbs, which was viewed as preferable to renting apartments in the city.[36] These prefabricated suburban tract homes were so affordable that even lower-class families could afford their very own homes. More and more people fled the expensive city life for quieter, more expansive suburban areas. With this focus on the nuclear family, recreation and leisure time became treasured family events that promoted togetherness, as well as demonstrated a family's wealth, making affordable amusements like the Saco Drive-In an easy way for families to participate in the new social construction of family time.

As the suburbs continued to grow, the demands for family-friendly entertainments increased. This idea of family and the emphasis on familial activities demonstrated society's attempt at bringing the family together, regardless of one's required activities (i.e. employment, education, et cetera) outside of the family unit.[37] Despite the popular media image of a domestic housewife, 60 percent of married women worked outside the home.[38] In a small town such as Saco, women worked in offices and shops along Main Street. Even the Saco Drive-In employed women to work at the ticket booth and in the concession stands. This late 1940s and 1950s family ideal gave rise to the familiar terms of "family room" and "family togetherness."

With suburbia developing into a warmer family environment as opposed to that offered by the city, a new idea of privacy and property emerged. This idea of privacy did not necessarily mean complete seclusion from one's neighbors but rather a sense of belonging to an exclusive community. This social cohesion, as described by Lynn Spigel, "allowed people to be together and alone by engaging the whole family in family based organization and amusements that gave people the freedom to keep their distance yet remain united under a wider social fabric."[39] Places like the Saco Drive-In merged private and public spaces and gave the family special time together while simultaneously being out in public as a unit. The drive-in also responded to the needs of a nuclear family unit with playgrounds, picnic tables and well-manicured lawn spaces that promoted organized family fun.

An advertisement from 1939 lists the drive-in theater as being located on Route 1 in Biddeford. This could be a printing error by the newspaper, or perhaps owners were attempting to get more traffic to the drive-in from people who lived in the smaller communities outside Biddeford, perhaps in Arundel or other surrounding areas.

Enjoying a Double Feature at the Saco Drive-In

The Saco Drive-In opened in 1939, six years after Hollingshead's Park-In Theater. Saco Drive-In's most known and loved owner, Eugene V. Boragine (1898–1961), was ten years old when his family immigrated to Queens, New York, from Naples, Italy, in 1909. According to census records, Boragine received only an eighth grade education and became a housepainter in his early adulthood. While in New York, he married Helen Toth (1902–1998).[40] The 1935 census lists the Boragines' residence as in Queens; however, only ten years later, Boragine moved to West Scarborough (now Saco) and opened the Motor-In Theater (now Saco Drive-In) on Route 1 in Saco.

Eugene Boragine in the Saco Drive-In snack bar, 1955. *Courtesy of David Priest.*

Boragine was not the first owner of the Saco Drive-In, as his obituary from 1961 lists him as the owner of the Saco Drive-In since 1947. According to usher Don Witham, who worked at the Saco Drive-In in 1947, Eugene Boragine initially had two other partners, one named O'Neil, who was regularly at the drive-in, and the other who was seldom present.

After three years, about 1950, Boragine bought out the other two men and tended to the drive-in himself, along with his wife. Boragine used his painting skills in the Saco Drive-In concession stand in the late 1940s or early 1950s. In the background of photographs inside the concession stand, a mural with what appear to be large palms can be seen. Boragine painted this mural himself around the whole stand.

Witham described Boragine as "a real family man" who enjoyed having lots of children and families attending movies at the drive-in. Later in his life, Boragine served as a deputy sheriff in addition to being the proprietor of the outdoor theater. Boragine died at the age of sixty-two on November 27, 1961.[41] According to Saco City records, the Saco Drive-In has changed owners only a few times, including being sold to the Hoyt's Cinema, which also operated the Portland Twin Drive-In located in Scarborough. The current owner of the Saco Drive-In property is Roberge Construction.

Eugene Boragine, circa 1950. *Courtesy of David Priest.*

Helen Boragine, wife of Eugene, at work in the concession stand in 1955. *Courtesy of David Priest.*

In a variety of advertisements during the early 1940s, the Motor-In Theater was identified as the "Auto Theater" or "Open Air Automobile Theater." This language is used to make it clear to newspaper readers that the Motor-In Theater was an entirely new form of entertainment for New England, Maine and the Saco area. But this new venture was short-lived. After the United States declared war on Japan in December 1941 and the government mandated blackout curtains for all households, in addition to the rubber and gasoline shortages, the Saco Drive-In closed for the duration of World War II. When the war ended, the theater reopened in July 1946. In the decade following the war, drive-ins spread across the United States. In less

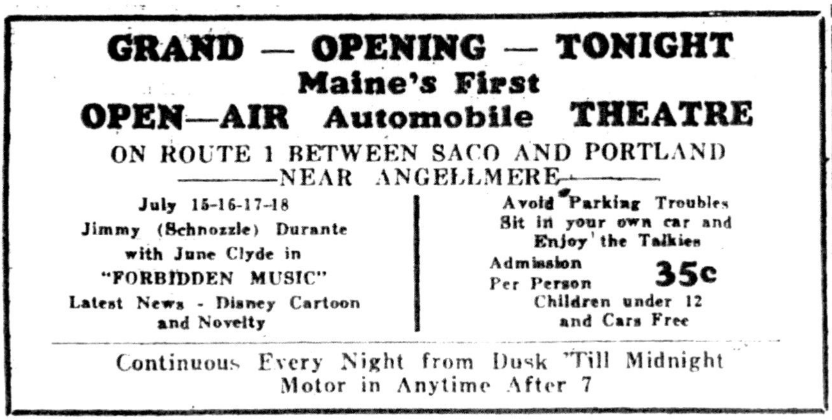

This advertisement states, "Near Angellmere," a restaurant nearby on Route 1 that served chicken and steak dinners. From the July 15, 1939 *Biddeford Daily Journal*. *McArthur Public Library Archives, Biddeford, Maine.*

than ten years, from 1946 through 1953, 2,976 drive-in theaters opened.[42] By 1957, Maine boasted 39 drive-in theaters, including the following still operational theaters: Pride's Corner, Westbrook (1953); Skowhegan Drive-In (1954); and the Twin Drive-In, Bridgton (1957). Also still operating is the Starlight Drive-In located in Madawaska, Maine, which opened significantly later than most drive-ins (1973). This rapid growth in drive-ins led Boragine to rename his Saco theater from the Motor-In to the Saco Motor-In Theater (1952) and then, in 1954, to the Saco Drive-In.[43]

In 1958, it is estimated that fifty million cars traveled the United States roadways.[44] This increase in automobile ownership contributed directly to the boom in drive-in growth, especially in Maine. Facing competition from so many drive-in theaters in the Southern Maine area (including Kennebunk, Sanford, Scarborough and Portland), Boragine renamed his drive-in theater twice in an effort to remain current and remind movie patrons, especially those who vacationed at Ocean Park or Old Orchard Beach during the summer, that the theater was outdoors and located in Saco. To keep the Saco Drive-In in the forefront of people's minds, Boragine's ticket booth staff gave out programs advertising the ozoner's weekly and weekend films.

Typically built on the outskirts of town, drive-ins often were surrounded by trees and set back from houses, much like the Saco Drive-In. Those who lived in neighborhoods off the Flag Pond Road and other northern Saco roads could hear the drive-in. Despite many complaints about the loud

Left: On the back of the screen in the 1950s, the large painted letters read, "Saco Open Air Automobile Theatre." Saco Drive-In Fountain. *Courtesy of David Priest.*

Below: A 1949 Saco Drive-In program inside view. *Courtesy of James Leary.*

Before or After the Show
Visit Maine's Finest

Dine *and* Dance
Spot

MALL LARRY'S ORCHESTRA

CHAR-LO-INN

Route 1 at Oak Hill
SCARBORO, MAINE

Fine Foods

Specials Daily—75c & up.

Tel. Scarboro 3358

SACO OPE
SACO,

Sunday - Monday - Tuesday
"APR
Jack Carson—
"WHO KIL
Virgini
"Mite Makes Right"

Wednesday - Thursday
"DE
Ida Lupino—
"A
F
"Pest Who Came To Dinner"

Friday - Saturday
"BI
Wayne Morris—I
"F
Walter
Cartoon **"T**

noise of the films and the increased lines of traffic along the shoulder of Route 1 before the gates opened, no ordinances or zoning laws were passed. However, not all drive-ins had such favorable locations. Many neighbors to less rural drive-in theaters complained about the loud noise from the films and claimed the sound could be heard clearly in their homes. Some towns passed ordinances regarding where ozoners could be constructed in an attempt to keep neighborhoods quiet and traffic at a minimum.[45] The theater owner could be sued by entire neighborhoods in some towns and charged with a misdemeanor if the film's sound could be heard fifty feet from the farthest property line.[46]

Clear sound proved to be a source of difficulty for the majority of drive-ins. Early drive-ins used one large speaker attached to the screen, which meant that the row of automobiles nearest to the speaker heard the sound first and the most clearly. RCA Victor Company, located in Camden, New Jersey, developed "Controlled Directional Sound," meaning that the theater had three central speakers and claimed everyone could hear the sound at

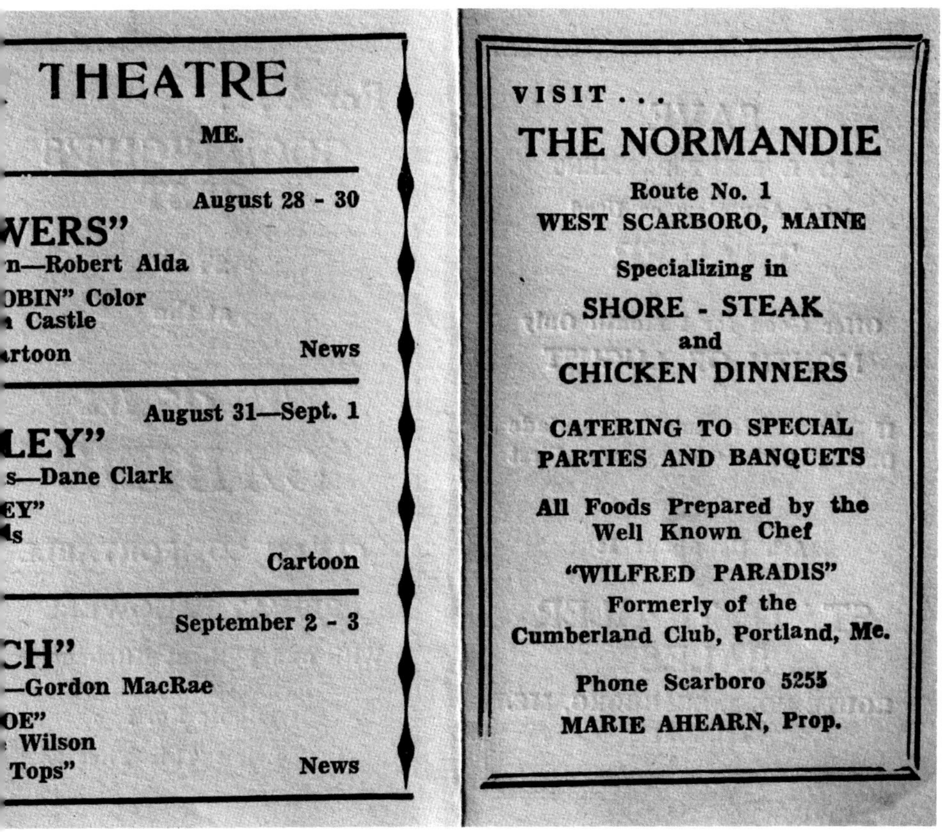

This image depicts the large growth of trees that still surrounds the Saco Drive-In as a way to keep out those patrons trying to sneak a peek at the latest films. *Postcard, circa 1960, from the author's private collection.*

once, which did not work out as advertised.[47] Drive-ins also experimented with ways to enhance the sound. One scheme involved grates under the parked cars, so the sound rose up from beneath the vehicles.[48] The Saco Drive-In used one large speaker until 1949, when the theater advertised "the New 1949 Streamlined Drive-In Theater." Boragine invested in a new, clearer screen and individual speakers that the drive-in staff placed inside each car. Movie patrons could easily control the volume themselves, which provided "greater listening pleasure." In addition to speakers, a variety of other products became commercialized as a result of their use at busy drive-in theaters. In-car heaters, popcorn machines and glycerin to keep rain off the windshield all became popular products that are still used today.[49] However, "car net" to keep pests out of the car while watching films with the windows down did not become a mainstream product. Interestingly, many servicemen and women have mentioned that mosquito netting did wonders for their drive-in experiences, yet the product did not seem to catch on in the 1950s.

Drive-ins often advertised themselves as a place to "avoid parking troubles" and "enjoy the talkies" for a lower price than indoor theaters.[50] Although today's drive-ins charge by the carload, early outdoor theaters

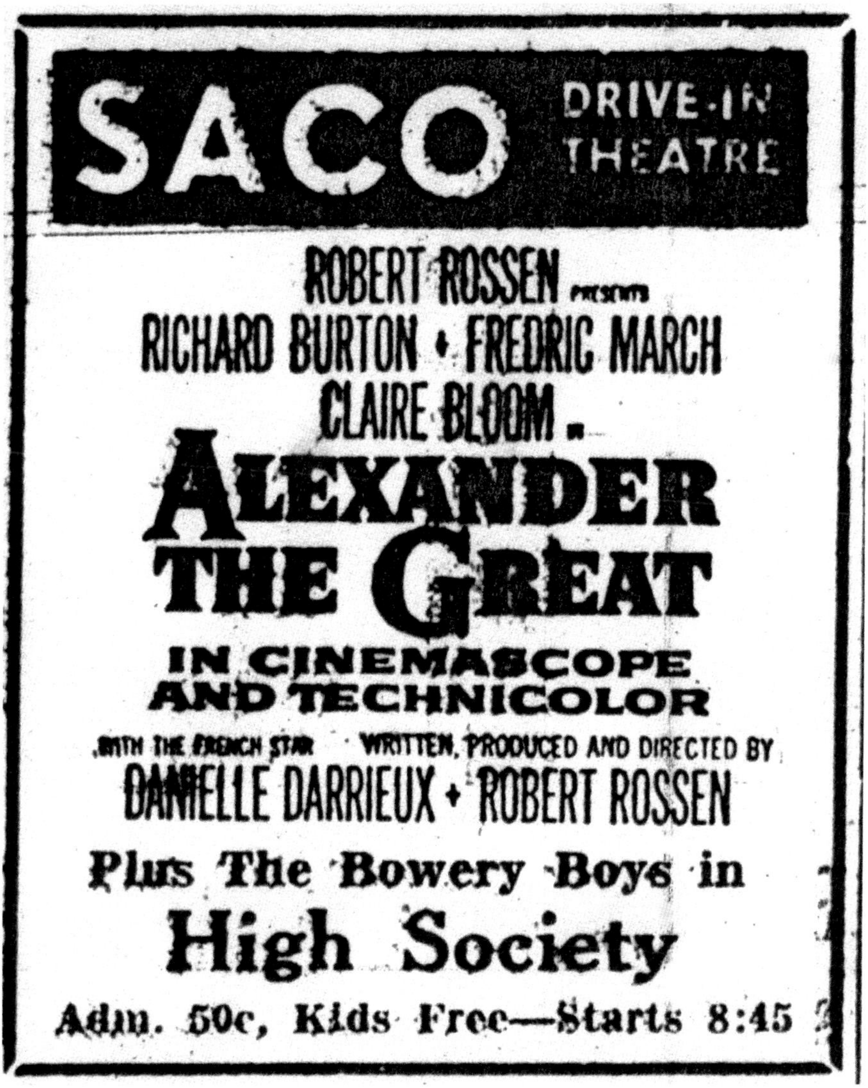

From the July 10, 1956 *Biddeford Daily Journal. McArthur Public Library Archives, Biddeford, Maine.*

charged per person for admission. On the Saco Drive-In's opening day, admission was thirty-five cents per person, and children twelve and under were free. By 1949, the price for adults had risen to fifty cents; by the 1960s, it was one dollar. This practice created a need to have extra staff at the box office to check for stowaway patrons hiding in the trunks of cars. The Saco

Drive-In tried to keep the practice of admitting children free for as long as was financially possible under the direction of Eugene Boragine. From the 1970s forward, it became easier for the drive-in staff to charge one fee per carload. This eliminated the need for extra staff and allowed patrons to all sit comfortably in the car while paying admission. In 2013, the ozoner charged fifteen dollars per carload with no limit on the number of people per car.

Drive-ins distinguished themselves from indoor theaters by emphasizing the unique ability to stay in one's own car, thus avoiding taking unruly children inside a traditional theater or being in a location that required Dad to put on a clean suit jacket after a long day at the office. Parents brought their children to the drive-in already in their pajamas, which allowed them to be tucked straight into bed after the film. The car represented an extension

From the August 3, 1939 *Biddeford Daily Journal. McArthur Public Library Archives, Biddeford, Maine.*

of the domestic space, a second living room, where families could gather together and enjoy time in a relaxed, informal setting.[51] After World War II, the ozoners became a space that readily accommodated wounded veterans, as sitting in a car was easier than navigating the small seats and tight aisles found within the indoor movie theater. The drive-in provided a welcoming atmosphere for families, veterans, couples and singles—all gathering to enjoy low-cost entertainment within the comfort of their own vehicles.

The Saco Drive-In, and others like it, often had trouble obtaining first-run films. Due to the rarity of first-rate films, the Saco Drive-In first showed the same film twice in one night, the last showing, as advertised, at 10:15 p.m. In the beginning, drive-in owners thought they could get more money and theater attendance by showing the same film up to three times in one evening. Instead, owners discovered the short exit time and entrance times caused major traffic jams, and the shows did not start on time. Unlike today, in the mid-twentieth century, films on their first runs were often available exclusively to Hollywood studio–owned indoor theaters. Drive-ins could choose between third- and fourth-run films at best or even much older films.[52]

From the October 7, 1939 *Biddeford Daily Journal. McArthur Public Library Archives, Biddeford, Maine.*

From the June 4, 1965 *Biddeford Daily Journal*. *McArthur Library Archives, Biddeford, Maine.*

As an example, the obscure film *The Love Life of a Gorilla* was released in 1937, making it three years old by the time it played at the Saco Drive-In. It could have been that the owners could not find a newer film for this particular run, as perhaps all the film reels were rented or on their first runs at nearby indoor theaters. During the 1940s, the Saco Drive-In often showed films that were three to five years old, but as the popularity of the theater increased, owners pushed back against major Hollywood film companies. The Supreme Court ruled that drive-in theaters could have access to first-run films. Despite this legal victory, obtaining first-rate films still proved difficult. When the ozoner carried first- and second-run films, the tagline "first area premiere" was added in many advertisements.[53]

In the late 1950s through the 1970s, drive-ins often showed less expensive, B-reel horror films. These films were less expensive to produce than standard big Hollywood features and enticed the younger generation to the drive-in. Directors in this genre, with exceedingly low budgets compared to big Hollywood films, geared these films toward the teenagers and other horror fans who enjoyed the outdoor experience. Many of these films involved invasions of humans by creatures from outer space, which cinema scholars believe represented the fear of the unknown and Communism during the

Cold War period. *Cry of the Banshee* is a prime example of a classic horror film starring the great Vincent Price, a notable character actor. According to film historian J. Rocky Colvito, "The makers of these films were not necessarily out to make the next *Citizen Kane*, nor were they targeting the discriminating film-goer with their product. Their target audience represented…teenagers and young adults who sought thrills, chills, and titillation."[54] These gory and sometimes sexual films allowed drive-in owners to give teenagers the films they wanted while still being able to show a double feature that included a more well-known film.

Newsreels and cartoons, in addition to special events like broadcasted boxing matches, often accompanied the features at the drive-in. On July 25, 1939, the Saco Drive-In drew crowds by screening the fight between Joe Lewis and "Two-Ton" Tony Galento. Children enjoyed Walt Disney's Mickey Mouse and other cartoons.[55] While the drive-in might not have had the first-run films, the theater showed the most current cartoons. As families owned radios and listened to the news and shows over the air, indoor and drive-in theaters showed newsreels so patrons could watch the news, or a cartoon, before the film.

In the 1960s, the Saco Drive-In proudly advertised that the theater always had *two* cartoons to accompany the feature film. As Beatlemania gripped the United States in the 1960s, the Saco Drive-In capitalized on the phenomenon by using the group's popularity as a way to gain attendance on a mid-week night. The film *A Hard Day's Night* had debuted only a month before, and the drive-in offered an outdoor environment where Beatles fans

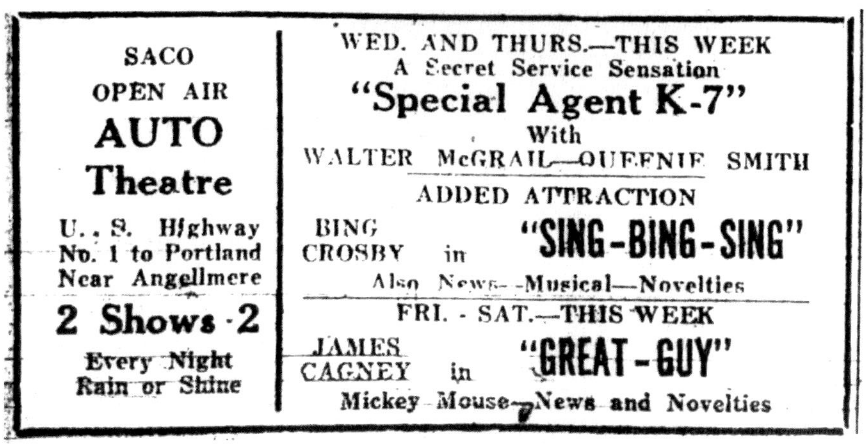

From the August 22, 1939 *Biddeford Daily Journal. McArthur Public Library Archives, Biddeford, Maine.*

From the August 11, 1964 *Biddeford Saco Journal*. *McArthur Public Library, Biddeford, Maine.*

could sing and dance with the film. The Saco Drive-In also participated in various patriotic events, like the Fourth of July, or celebrating the twentieth anniversary of World War II's D-Day with a special showing of *The Longest Day*. To keep the smallest patrons entertained, many theaters installed playgrounds for children to use before or even during the show. The Saco Drive-In featured two playgrounds: one under the screen and another behind the current concession stand. The variety of activities allowed parents to let their children, who might have had little interest in the film, get out of the car and play.

In addition to playgrounds, ozoners often offered a variety of other amusements, including dance floors and variety shows; ironically, some even installed small televisions for patrons to watch. As drive-in theaters frequently played older films, drive-in owners used every possible type of amusement to get patrons to the theater early and keep them there.[56] A theater in Asbury Park, New Jersey, advertised "Fly-in, drive-in," as patrons with their own planes could land at the airstrip that adjoined the theater and taxi closer to the screen to enjoy the film.[57] However, this airstrip drive-in was quite an anomaly among theaters.

Drive-in owners believed that patrons who arrived early to the theater would purchase more concessions. In addition to the playground, the Saco Drive-In had a dance floor for patrons to enjoy before the double feature started. Drive-ins also created special picnic areas for families to eat

Sitting at the fountain, circa 1958. *Courtesy of David Priest.*

together—preferably enjoying refreshments purchased from the concession stand. Behind the screen at the Saco Drive-In, remnants of a park can still be seen. At the entrance of the theater, deer and polar bears with a large fountain greeted guests (one deer is still visible). A picnic light is still located on the perimeter, and one picnic table remains. Some theaters experimented with adding covered outdoor seating for those patrons who did not drive or did not wish to sit in their car.[58]

Concession stands at early outdoor theaters offered a limited selection of popcorn and soda. However, as the films often began late in the evening, owners quickly realized they could make more money with larger menus (similar to indoor theaters today). As pizza was not quite a popular food item yet, those drive-ins that sold it often had patrons who paid the admission fee to the drive-in just to buy a slice.[59] The Saco Drive-In sold hot dogs at the ticket booth and allowed non-film patrons to walk up and buy treats without paying admission. As concessions took off, patrons were soon able to purchase hot dogs, hamburgers and French fries in addition to soda and popcorn. Some theaters offered fried chicken or baskets of fried fish, depending on the geographic location.[60] Candy, including licorice and penny candy, as well as Cracker Jacks, ice cream cups and taffy apples, also became popular snacks.

By the mid-1950s, food was not the only available item at the concession stands. Adult patrons purchased cigarettes, tissues, aspirin or batteries for flashlights in

Shirley Davis, 1955, in the storeroom behind the concession stands. This room is still used for snack storage today. *Courtesy of David Priest.*

Saco Drive-In Snack Bar, 1980. *Courtesy of David Priest.*

addition to snacks, while their children purchased comic books such as *The Lone Ranger*, *Batman* and *Superman*. The snack bar at the Saco Drive-In is located in the middle of the ozoner, surrounded by a white picket fence. In the 1950s, picnic tables surrounded the stand, and there was a playground behind it. According to Don Whitham, there was another snack bar to the right of the concession stand, which perhaps was turned into the Saco Drive-In cottage used by David Priest in the 1980s. Snack bars were heavily promoted in the 1950s, with special trailers running before and during intermission featuring dancing hot dogs, ice cream and other items. These trailers were often produced by Filmack Studios.[61] Armour Hotdogs produced one-minute-long advertisements.[62] By expanding the offerings at the concession stands, drive-ins made more money to help offset the high price of films.

Many outdoor theater owners blamed the television, radio and multiplex cinemas for stagnated drive-in attendance throughout the 1960s. According to historian Lynn Spigel, as television became more accessible and affordable, it created "a substitute community" and contributed to "the decline of traditional community life."[63] Just as novels and other literature of the nineteenth century produced armchair travelers, the television, with new programs and news reports from all over the globe, gave individuals a chance

From the September 9, 1970 *Biddeford Daily Journal. McArthur Library Archives, Biddeford, Maine.*

to experience a wider world within their own living rooms (much like Internet and on-demand information in the twenty-first century). Usually located in the family's main living space, the television became a source of family togetherness without them having to leave the home. By the mid-1960s, most drive-ins saw attendance numbers in steady decline. With a shrinking revenue stream, owners resorted to and continued to show older, cheaper, B-reel films, including the now classic drive-in horror films. Film historian Gary Rhodes describes this phenomenon as the "novelty of the drive-in wearing off," and drive-ins competed against one another to get decent films; thus "the drive-in horror, which may or may not have been intended for hardtops [indoor theaters]...were primarily seen at ozoners."[64] By 1969, George A. Romero's *Night of the Living Dead* was seen in drive-ins across America, cementing the theaters' notoriety for horror films.[65] In 1970, the Saco Drive-In screened the newly released *Equinox* with *Night of the Living Dead.*

The 1970s saw a rapid decline in the number of drive-in theaters, while twice as many shut their gates permanently in the 1980s.[66] During the energy crisis and economic recession of the 1970s, gas rationing took effect across

The Saco Drive-In tantalized horror fans and teenagers with films such as *Race with the Devil.* From the July 10, 1975 *Biddeford Daily Journal. McArthur Library Archives, Biddeford, Maine.*

the country. Unlike during World War II when theaters closed, drive-ins still ran double features, often to half-filled or less theaters. As fewer people could afford gas, many could not justify using gas to drive to the drive-in and potentially spending even more money there. To reduce gas consumption, the United States government imposed national maximum speeds of fifty-five miles per hour on all major roadways, which included Interstate 95 to and from Maine, as well as Route 1. Due to the shortage of fuel, the tourism industry in Maine suffered.[67] Visitors were not motoring in to Old Orchard Beach and other amusements in the high numbers of years past.

As drive-in owners failed to sell tickets, more and more drive-in gates closed permanently in the 1980s. In Maine, many drive-ins, including those in Windham, Kennebunk and Sanford, among others, were padlocked permanently, and the properties went up for sale. The Saco Drive-In managed to stay open while many drive-in theaters closed, despite showing gory, occasionally obscure and sometimes older films. With the lacking attendance and income, theater owners could not afford to pay the high rental fees to

From the July 24, 1981 *Biddeford Daily Journal*. *McArthur Library Archives, Biddeford, Maine.*

bring first-run films or more mainstream films to the cinema until their third or fourth runs—similar to the issues drive-in owners faced in the 1950s.

In an effort to fill the stalls, theater owners resorted to double and sometimes triple features of R-rated and soft-core pornographic films. Many of the Saco Drive-In's later advertisements in the 1980s reflect this shift in film selections. In addition to less-mainstream films, throughout the 1980s, the Saco Drive-In used soft-core pornographic films to draw crowds. More than one Saco citizen commented on the "dirty" films shown at the drive-in. In the 1950s, revenue streamed into the drive-in as people clamored to pull in and get a good spot to watch films. By 1980, even with adult films on the marquee, the drive-in could barely make ends meet. Some theaters experienced protests by fundamentalist groups that attempted to sue owners for showing adult films. However, the Supreme Court ruled that such films are protected under the First Amendment, and drive-in owners could not be sued.[68] Despite such lean times, the Saco Drive-In managed to survive.

From the August 28, 1981 *Biddeford Daily Journal. McArthur Library Archives, Biddeford, Maine.*

Saco Drive-In from Route 1, 1980. *Courtesy of David Priest.*

Back of the Saco Drive-In screen, 1980. *Courtesy of David Priest.*

By the 1980s, the look of the Saco Drive-In had changed, as had Route 1, or the Portland Road, itself. Unlike the entrance to the theater of the 1960s, now a large, standard marquee replaced the big, lighted arrow. Many people remember the original marquee, but rumor has it that the sign was broken during one of the many Maine winter storms in the late 1970s. In 1955, the back of the screen was painted: "Open Air Automobile Theater." By the 1980s, the back of the screen read, "Saco Drive-In Theatre." Currently, very tall trees grow in front of the screen, and the faint remnants of this paint can be viewed only by standing in front of the garden space.

Unlike the 1950s cabins, restaurants with shore dinners, thicker trees and brush and other amusements that once lined the road, large automobile dealerships have purchased expansive lots and often demolished structures that were previously on the property. Cinemagic theaters, a New England movie theater chain, also purchased a large piece of land for a multiplex and, later, built an IMAX addition. Many people know Saco's "auto mile"; however, this is not for the Saco Drive-In but rather for the section of Route 1 with a high concentration of car dealerships and auto mechanics. Currently, there are a few motels and cabins, but mostly banks, stores and a few amusements dot the landscape. Most tourists in the twenty-first century prefer to be steps away from

From the May 24, 1956 *Biddeford Daily Journal. McArthur Public Library Archives, Biddeford, Maine.*

the beach or vacation in Old Orchard Beach proper or larger cities like Portland. Along Route 1, across from the Saco Drive-In, is Aquaboggan, a water park that opened in the late 1970s as the economy began to rebound. By and large, Route 1 from Saco to Scarborough in the twenty-first century is for businesses and auto dealerships.

As the changes in the physical landscape occurred, so did changes in theater technology. In the 1950s, indoor theaters used Cinemascope, a clearer, higher-quality sound system that was unattainable for drive-in theaters. However, by the mid-1950s, drive-in theaters could install and use Cinemascope. A 1955 film starring decorated World War II veteran Audie Murphy boasted the use of Cinemascope, most likely for the sounds during intense battle scenes. In the 2000s, indoor theaters switched to an all-digital film projection format. For large multiplex and chain cinemas like Regal or Cinemagic, the financial burden of installing $75,000 digital projectors could be easier to bear with round film sales and multiple locations with steady incomes. However, for a small, single-screen drive-in theater that is only open from May to October (weather permitting), the cost of a digital projector could close the theater permanently. Hollywood film production companies produced only a handful of movies on film reels, making the films more expensive and harder to obtain, nearly impossible to get on a first run. Drive-in theaters, once again, fought to get first-run films and access to more pictures. In the late 2000s, the Saco Drive-In was up for lease, just waiting for a new manager to come bring fresh energy.

Twenty-First-Century Technology Threatens the Old Theater

In 2010, Ry Russell took over management of the Saco Drive-In and leased the theater for the season. After two seasons, and as film selection dwindled, Russell knew the theater had to make the digital conversion to remain a viable business. As the theater recovered from the stagnation in the 1980s to showing more first-run films in the 1990s, there was no going back to showing older films. Russell put together a small committee in hopes of jumpstarting fundraising for a $75,000 new digital projector. The committee met to discuss strategy and plans to move forward with pledges and approached larger businesses with a plan for advertising on a new digital projector. As the committee entered the 2013 season and organized various fundraising events for the summer, automaker Honda approached Russell in July with "Project Drive-In."

Honda's "Project Drive-In" involved giving away five digital projectors to the top five drive-ins in the United States. In 2013, fewer than three hundred drive-ins existed across the country, and after the digital conversion, that number would be decreased by half. To accomplish its goal of giving away digital projectors, Honda set up a website for the competition, and each drive-in received its own page to promote itself with a video, a paragraph of information and photographs of the theater. Honda filmed several promotional pieces for the project, including a few at the Saco Drive-In that featured state representative Justin Chenette, myself and Ry Russell talking about the importance of the drive-in theater as a family amusement. The competition went live on August 9 and ran for thirty days, concluding on September 9. Film fans could vote for one drive-in daily, via text or social media.

The Saco Drive-In staff and supporters got right to work and promoted the theater, utilizing its vast social media following. The fundraising team and drive-in patrons shared the "Project Drive-In" links daily and encouraged friends, acquaintances and family members to vote for the theater as America's Top Drive-In.

The local media, including the *Portland Press Herald*, the *Journal Tribune* and other Saco, Biddeford and Scarborough papers, supported the Saco Drive-In. Kate Irish Collins, a reporter for the *Sun Chronicle*, a local Saco and Biddeford paper, covered the Saco Drive-In's initial struggle for funding. The article featured manager Ry Russell with photographs of the film projector, so large that it took up nearly the entire projection room. The *Courier*, another local Saco and Biddeford newspaper, also covered the Saco Drive-In's need for funding. As the summer progressed, a variety of websites and blogs posted articles and thoughts about the Honda Project and the need to save the Saco Drive-In. The Maine Historical Society posted a blog about saving the past and how important the drive-in is, particularly linking Maine's first drive-in, the Saco Drive-In, to a wider American narrative of life after World War II and the age of the automobile. Smalley and Chenette, along with Maggie Oliver, planned a large yard sale at the Saco Drive-In. Patrons donated items to be sold, and vendors could purchase space and sell their goods as well. Russell also rented a blow-up bounce house for the children who came with their parents, and the snack bar was open all day. Smalley managed a table of Saco Drive-In merchandise, as well as many silent auction items donated by local businesses. At the end of a hot summer day, the yard sale made about $2,000, a good amount for a day's worth of work but not enough to put the Saco Drive-In much closer to purchasing a digital projector.

Many generous patrons offered to host bake sales at the theater, and others donated proceeds from food trucks in an effort to help the theater and get the word out. Russell and Chenette filmed YouTube videos promoting the theater and reminding everyone to vote for the Saco Drive-In, both by text message and on Facebook. Word kept spreading, and posts were shared by individuals and businesses alike. The Southern Maine community rallied behind Maine's oldest drive-in theater in an effort to prove the second-oldest still-operating drive-in was indeed America's best.

The thirty days from August until September proved to be a long sprint for the Saco Drive-In supporters. Honda announced on September 9 that it would reveal one drive-in per day as a winner. On September 12, Honda contacted Russell and declared the Saco Drive-In Theater the number one drive-in and the first winner of a digital projector. The news stunned the fundraising committee. The Saco Drive-In, a small theater in Maine, a state with a population that is smaller than that of other drive-in cities, won the top slot. Winning the digital projector meant the Saco Drive-In would not close its gates at the end of the 2014 season, when Hollywood ceased producing film reels. That evening, a huge celebration took place at the theater, with news crews, reporters and hundreds of eager Saco Drive-In patrons in attendance. Honda announced the next four drive-in winners and then added an additional four, for a total of nine saved drive-ins. Just as drive-ins struggled historically to gain equal footing with indoor theaters in the face of changing technology in the mid-twentieth century, the Saco Drive-In managed to stay on top in the second round of that battle.

The city of Saco has survived changes in technology and economy since the seventeenth century, and the Saco Drive-In endured the boom of the 1950s through the rapid decline of the 1980s and still showed films for carloads of movie fans, both local Saco residents and out-of-state guests. Although the drive-in no longer has a playground, dance floor or picnic area, patrons still flock to watch double features on the big screen. The Saco Drive-In still offers the family-friendly atmosphere patrons sought in earlier years. Parents, often nostalgic for their own childhood experiences at the drive-in, still bring their children for movie nights. Often, children, still clad in pajamas, stand and play catch with their parents while waiting for the movie to start. A staple of Saco recreation for generations of visitors, the Saco Drive-In is a treasured piece of American culture and remains a classic place for families to watch films and enjoy one another's company.

Feature 2

MEMORIES OF THE SACO DRIVE-IN

(As Told by Patrons)

"Screen." *Courtesy of Charlie Widdis Photography©.*

Bud Priest, 1955, at work in the concession stand, probably going to hang a new movie poster for an upcoming feature. *Courtesy of David Priest.*

Lilla Priest, 1955, behind the counter of the concession stands. *Courtesy of David Priest.*

David Priest, Massachusetts

I was involved with Saco Drive-In from 1955 (as a small boy) through the mid-1980s, when SBC sold the drive-in. I went to movies there as a boy while my parents worked. All of my brothers (Carl, Frank, Bill) worked there as teenagers, working in the snack bar, doing "ramp duty" (turning off speakers, making repairs, parking cars on busy nights and doing car-to-car canister collections for the Jimmy Fund). In the summer of 1969, my brother Bill managed the snack bar. The drive-in was managed by Mr. Ernie Hughes that summer. At some point, Mr. Boragine sold out to Lockwood and Gordon Theaters. As a boy, I vividly recall walking around the grounds at both Portland and Saco Drive-Ins placing little white stickers on all the speakers, identifying them as the Property of L&G Theaters and the fine for stealing or driving off with one of the speakers. Then there were times that my father would park our car in one of the back rows prior to the start of the movie or when I would hide in the woods behind the drive-in near the "moon" pole so I could spy on people sneaking into the drive-in with paying people who would hide in the trunk of a car or try to sneak in on foot through the woods.

During the 1960s, my father worked at nearby Portland Drive-In as the snack bar manager. My brothers and I all worked there at various times doing odd jobs like mowing lawns, snack bar, selling tickets, fixing speakers, et cetera. Those duties often took us to Saco Drive-In. We also did what was called the "Circus Poster Route." My father would prepare weekly advertising posters with current movie selections at both Portland and Saco Drive-Ins. My brothers and I would place the posters in store windows, campgrounds, motels, chamber of commerce office and tourist information locations and billboards in the Saco/Old Orchard Beach area, leaving two free movie passes for every poster placed. My father eventually became the full-time manager at Portland Twin Drive-In. He retired in 1979. I left my job as a retail store manager in Vermont and became the manager of Portland Twin Drive-In.

The company (Boston-based SBC Management Corporation), which had purchased the drive-ins from Lockwood and Gordon, allowed me to move into the cottage at Saco Drive-In as part of my salary. In 1980, I became the manager of both Portland and Saco Drive-Ins. Later that year, I became the district manager of Maine and New Hampshire supervising drive-in theaters in Auburn, Lewiston, Winslow, Skowhegan and indoor cinemas in Waterville, Farmington and Newington, New Hampshire. The office at Saco Drive-In, located between the box office and the screen tower, became my district office. On September 19, 1981, my wife, Marion, and I were

Dave and Marion Priest at their wedding reception inside the cottage at the Saco Drive-In. *Courtesy of David Priest.*

Opposite: The cottage at the Saco Drive-In. *Courtesy of David Priest.*

married in the cottage at Saco Drive-In. We lived in the cottage for six years with our daughter, Peggy, and our golden retriever, Taffy. Peggy and I used to play basketball on the patio in front of the cottage, and Taffy and I used to go for runs around the drive-in perimeter.

As the drive-in business began to decline, my focus turned to bigger, more profitable indoor theaters, and my territory expanded to the west, reaching Rochester, New York.*

* The snack bar is located in the middle of the drive-in, surrounded by a white picket fence. In the 1950s, picnic tables surrounded the stand, as well as a playground behind it. According to Don Witham, there was another snack bar to the right of the concession stand, which perhaps was turned into the Saco Drive-In cottage used by David Priest in the 1980s. One by one, the drive-ins were closed and sold off as the property became more valuable as real estate. Much of the technology behind the filming and production of motion pictures—like stereo sound and visual special effects—did not come across as well at drive-ins as it did at darkened indoor cinemas. Then there was increasing competition from cable television, HBO, computers, et cetera, which vied for entertainment dollars. America's appetite for film also changed, and the 1930s/'40s/'50s era of family entertainment began to change. The magic that once brought to the drive-in families with their children in pajamas and young people with their dates became a point of nostalgia.

I don't recall whom SBC sold Saco Drive-In to. My office was moved to the Cines 8 location in Biddeford and eventually to Massachusetts, where I now live.

I retired from the movie business in 2007 after a very rewarding and entertaining career in the motion picture industry. However, the most fun I ever had in any job was during those six years when I lived and worked at Saco Drive-In.

Ry Russell, Saco Drive-In Manager, Scarborough, Maine

I chose to run the drive-in, as it was something my family did with my sister and I as kids. We did not have a lot of money growing up, so we didn't really go on vacations; we would go to the drive-in. Honestly, some of my favorite memories as a child…I knew how much it meant to my parents. Kids see everything, so I remember fondly a day that my dad didn't know I was there, and he was worried about paying bills, and a few hours later when my mom got home from work they packed us up and took us to the theater; they were laughing, and it was like we were in a different world where nothing mattered. I know so many families have these same stories, and I wanted to make sure the drive-in stayed open for those people.

In February 2011, when my dad and I drove past the Saco Drive-In on Route 1 with the For Lease sign, he told me I should lease it and run it. I thought he was insane but knew that I could do this. I knew that I could take the Saco Drive-In, which had been for lease for quite some time at this point, and make it great. All the Saco Drive-In truly needed was good marketing and a fresh perspective to restore the theater to the popularity it once had in the 1950s. I think families want more together time and value entertainments that allow the whole family, teenagers and younger children included, to enjoy the evening. It is not easy in 2014 to find something that pleases everyone and is affordable—that's a rarity. In the 1950s, drive-in patrons sought quality family time for a low cost, and that's the same thing families sixty-four years later want and I'm sure families in another fifty years will still want. Truthfully, I wanted to give back to the community by running the Saco Drive-In and take an active stewardship of a place that is a fond memory for me. I wanted children to experience the Saco Drive-In and, in twenty years, experience the same happy nostalgia that I do, my parents do and grandparents as well.

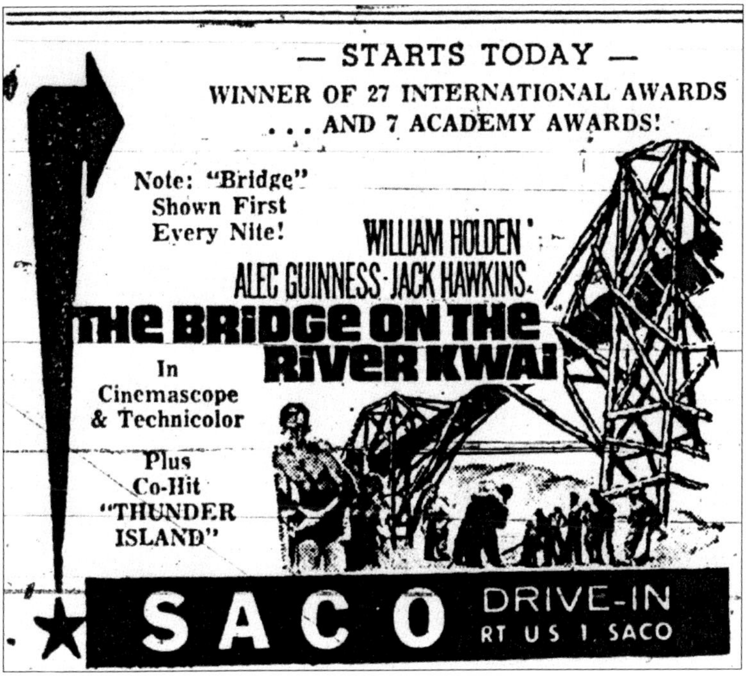

From the May 25, 1964 *Biddeford Daily Journal. McArthur Public Library Archives, Biddeford, Maine.*

While I very much enjoy running the Saco Drive-In, it's very much like running two different businesses. While on one hand, I have to manage receiving the films, which when we used a film-based projector, sometimes I would drive as far as Augusta or Portsmouth to get a film reel. As the 2012 season progressed, it became much harder to get films on their first run in an attempt to compete with Cinemagic and other indoor theaters. The standard way of receiving movies starts by negotiating with the movie companies the terms by which we will rent the movies, which is usually on a percentage basis—which can be sometimes as high as 90 percent—so it is definitely a challenge. Once we come to an agreement, which is more of them telling us what we are paying than a real negotiation, they shipped them to us on reels, and then we put them together on a big platter as one reel. This is very similar to the way the Saco Drive-In received their films in the 1950s. I heard from a few older patrons that the original owner actually knew someone in the film industry and was able to get better films on their first run. It's remarkable to me how drive-ins have basically fought the same battle for film rights for the past seventy-five years.

The film projector at the Saco Drive-In actually isn't the original projector. This projector is from an old drive-in that was located in another area in Maine. The Saco Drive-In got it in the 1990s as the older projector failed to work. What I think was really cool, and a great marketing strategy that played to the history of drive-ins, was Honda's use of the long arrow–styled drive-in advertisement for their posters. This style of 1960s marketing is classic, and Honda did a great job capitalizing on the nostalgia of drive-ins to really get the word out that, once again, drive-ins are facing a hardship, and this time, it's projection. Thanks to Honda, we have the digital projector. Now the standard for the digital projector has a few different options, either via satellite or portable hard drive. With either one of these methods, we will be able to run films as soon as they're available, meaning no more competing with a broker against other drive-ins or other theaters.

When I took over this theater, I really wanted to implement a good, strong marketing strategy that put the Saco Drive-In back on the map. So the strategy is actually very simple: our customers do the talking, and we do our best to allow people the freedom to enjoy the theater the way they want to enjoy it. If they have a good time, they are going to keep bringing their friends and family—and that is the important piece. Of course, I utilize

"Snack time." *Courtesy of Charlie Widdis Photography©*.

standard media like radio advertisements to make sure everyone in the Southern Maine community knows what movies are playing and remind them we have delicious treats at concessions.

The second half of the drive-in business is concessions and running basically a small restaurant. Like drive-in owners before me, the concession stand is really where you are going to please patrons. This is going to help make or break your theater. If you have terrible concessions and bad food—who wants to go to your theater? I have to be diligent about what I choose for food. I have found that running specials, like fried dough, for a few evenings tends to be profitable over having it year round. You want people to enjoy your product and not get sick of it, particularly for those families who come here every other weekend. Unlike previous owners in the 1950s, pizza is very popular now and easily one of our top-selling items. What I find to be ironic—indoor movie theaters like Cinemagic also push concessions. I think it probably was the drive-in that really pushed the idea of more food than just popcorn, and everyone else picked up on it. Now you can get almost anything you can think of. As the cost of film rental is so high, you need concessions to make the business work.

To really make this business work, I knew we needed to purchase a digital projector. It became so difficult to get films at the end of the 2012 season, I knew we had to get the projector—had to. It was a life-or-death situation for the theater. Many people suggested to me, "Oh, well, you can just show older films." That's a really great theory and an idea; however, it's not a reality. Showing older films was not going to fill the theater every night. Instead, the Saco Drive-In would probably only be open on Saturday evenings and show a double feature of an older film. This probably wouldn't fill the theater enough to even pay three of my staff members. Instead, I knew we needed to have the digital projector. I organized a fundraising committee with hopes that we could, somehow, raise $75,000 for a new digital projector. We had very lofty goals, but I felt certain that Camille, Justin and I, along with Maggie Oliver and a few others, could make this happen. We planned a few events, silent auctions, a Kickstarter campaign and a couple different strategies for getting the word out about the theater needing the digital projector. We made about $5,000 by June, but we had only three and a half months, at best, to finish this and find $70,000 more. When Honda called me about Project Drive-In, I was elated. It was our shot, and I was going to take it. I was going to run hard with this for the whole campaign—I knew we were going to win. Saco people are passionate about their community, and we had real spirit behind us. We really utilized social media to promote the drive-in during Project Drive-In. People who "liked" our page promoted the drive-in; members of the fundraising committee, staff and their parents all promoted the drive-in. The amount of support I received, phone calls and everything, was wild. It was a month-long sprint. The interesting thing about Project Drive-In to me is, we are utilizing the very technology that started to close drive-ins. Being able to watch a film at home, on your Smartphone, streaming almost wherever you are—that Internet and television is what started to close the theaters in the 1960s—and here we are, using it to save the Saco Drive-In. I cannot express how glad I am that we did save the drive-in, not just as my business but as that classic Saco icon on historic Route 1.

Justin Chenette, State Representative, Saco, Maine

When the owner of the Saco Drive-In came to me [in] early winter 2012 with the bad news that this next upcoming summer season could be its last, I knew we had to do something. The Saco Drive-In is not just a regional job creator but a cultural pillar to our community's rich dynamic history. The film industry, in order to save a buck, was forcing mom and pop drive-ins across the country to convert to digital-only films or no-go on showing the latest movie. On paper it might have looked like a good idea for them, but in reality, who really has $80,000-plus for a digital projector lying around? Not small drive-ins like here in Saco, that's for sure.

At first there were major doubts. In fact, throughout this ten-month journey, there were doubts not just from the public but ourselves as well. How could we get the money needed in time? Could we really save our beloved drive-in? We launched a massive effort to fundraise online and through events. We were on every TV station, in every newspaper, on every radio show we could possibly do to raise awareness. A few hundred dollars here, a few thousand dollars there, but we weren't anywhere near our total by the start of what could have been the last season. We were nervous.

It just so happened that the Honda Motor Company was preparing to launch a national contest to give away a few digital projectors to drive-ins through an online voting competition. Perfect timing. It felt as if this was a sign and validation for all the work done up to that point. Like

Christmas day—a gift was just laid before our feet. It wasn't a done deal, though. We had to compete with drive-in theaters that had populations in their area ten times the size of our whole state. We were up against the big guys. Once again, there were those that doubted we could pull it off. There wasn't a day that went by that any one of us didn't contemplate what would happen if we lost. This was the final push. If we didn't win this contest, the drive-in would close and be lost to future generations to enjoy and make memories.

I don't think any of us slept during the month of the voting for the contest. It was the top priority for all of us. We ate, breathed and slept drive-in contest promotions. VOTE. VOTE. VOTE. It almost felt [like] we were managing a political campaign, asking for votes instead of financial donations that we were previously. When all it takes is a click of your mouse to help save our drive-in, it takes on a whole new meaning. People acted in large numbers. Not just in Saco but all across Maine and even New England. Families, students, seniors—every age group got involved that was ever touched in some way [by] the drive-in.

This was community organizing at its best. People took to Twitter to retweet. People shared our "Save the drive-in" postings almost every day. This was a strong extended community effort. It really demonstrated how much this place meant to people. It was and is so much more than just a business. It's a piece of our community. It's a piece of our lives.

SACO
OPEN-AIR
THEATRE
Portland Road
Near Angellmere

LAST TIME TONIGHT
Sally Rand in "Sunset Murder Case"
and "Titans of the Deep"
Plus News and Cartoon

SUN., MON., TUES.—2 BIG FEATURES—2
A Riot of Fun with MARY BOLAND in
"MAMA RUNS WILD"
She Tried To Boss the Whole Town and ???
Also the Highest Note in Musical Entertainment
BUDDY ROGERS In "DANCE BAND"
JUNE CLYDE
Stars—Girls—Comedy—Music
Plus CARTOON and LATEST NEWS EVENTS

Owners added the tagline of "Stars-Girls-Comedy-Music" to attract all potential moviegoers. From the September 16, 1939 *Biddeford Daily Journal. McArthur Public Library Archives, Biddeford, Maine.*

The day we discovered we were the first drive-in to win one of the digital projectors was surreal, to say the least. I wanted someone to pinch me because I thought I was dreaming. Are you sure? Was this a prank? Nope, it was real all right, and Honda officials were there that day to let us know in person. I felt like collapsing on the ground, half to fall asleep from exhaustion but the other half to cry tears of joy. After all that we went through, it was all worth it in the end. We saved it. Together. Each and every one of us. Maine showed the nation: you don't mess with us. We are one big family that looks after one another. Mainers band together in times of need for support, and this was a prime example of that persistence in the face of adversity. Moral of the story: never give up.

I'm over the moon that our Saco Drive-In will be around as a constant connector to our past and an opportunity for future generations to enjoy making memories with their loved ones in our beautiful Maine summers for many years to come.

Nicholas Jordan, Maine

I went to the Saco Drive-In in the early 2000s with my parents during the summer season. I think I was eight to ten years old at the time. I was a very artistic child (still am as an adult) and very much enjoyed coloring and drawing. I often sat outside during the summer and drew what I saw around me. I also liked to draw characters I saw on television and movies, especially things from *Star Wars*. I designed new droids for Luke; I often drew characters from *Star Wars* like Luke, Leia and Han. Later, when *Episode I* came out, I started drawing those droids and other new characters. Anakin and I were about the same age, so it was really fun to imagine my life as a Jedi Padawan and then draw it. When I saw *Star Wars, Episode II* at the Saco Drive-In, it was one of the best memories I have. My parents did not really want to see the film, but they wanted to see the film after it, which worked out well for us. Even better, sitting in the car, I could sit with my drawing book and draw as I watched the movie, just like at home. No one was bothered by my flashlight, so I could see what I was doing. Munching popcorn, watching *Star Wars* and drawing—it was the highlight of my childhood. Even now, I am curious about the new *Star Wars* films and hope that the Saco Drive-In will be open and able to show them when they come out in 2015. Perhaps the drive-in could even have some sort of *Star Wars* party event!

Mark Johnston, Former Saco Mayor, Saco, Maine

When I was a kid in the 1960s, I worked at the Saco Drive-In, as did my brother and my mother. I helped take admissions and check the cars for stowaway movie fans that thought they could pass undetected in the trunk of the car. I also checked the cars, assisted with sound issues and sometimes stayed in the projection room. I was there in the mid-1960s, so I never met the original owner of the theater or his wife. That was a great summer job, however. Hanging out at the theater, outside in the summer air, and making some small amount of money—which was helpful. As someone who grew up in Saco and enjoys Saco's history, the Saco Drive-In is a major piece of Saco's twentieth-century [experience]. It fits right in with the national narrative of expanding roadways, skyrocketing population, new technology such as cars and new leisure activities such as film.

Since the town's inception, Saco has been an area with a growing economic base and a growing population. People have always been drawn to this area, be it the rush of the falls as a source of economic vitality, the fishing industry, the beautiful beaches off Saco Bay or even the growing downtown. In the twenty-first century, people are still drawn to the Saco area, not for textile factories and railroad stations but to raise families and enjoy the scenery. Much like in the late nineteenth century, people still summer at Camp Ellis, rent cottages on Ferry Road and enjoy conferences and other gatherings at the Ferry Beach Park Association. Saco is a real place for people to slow down and enjoy life, which is exactly what the Saco Drive-In offers. People started going to the Saco Drive-In in 1939 to take time for themselves, to enjoy their families, to take a moment and enjoy the sweet summer air that's only available for four months of the year. The same concerns for families in 1939 are very similar in 2013. Cost, location, genuine interaction with each other—all things that are on people's minds. One location has given people a wholesome family adventure for a low price in a convenient location for seventy-five years, and that is Saco's very own drive-in theater.

Alicia Pelletier, Saco Drive-In Patron

I voted so many times for the Saco Drive-In during Project Drive-In! I shared the link almost every day and reminded people to vote, both via text and the website. I don't think many people realize how important the Saco Drive-In is. It's been in Saco for seventy-four years. That's definitely one of the oldest

"Popcorn." *Photograph by Charlie Widdis Photography©.*

businesses in Saco. I always bring my kids to the drive-in during the summer months. It's so much easier to pack the car with all the toys and other items they need than to worry about hauling it into the indoor theater. This is the place my kids love, and I love bringing them here. I am so happy the Saco Drive-In won the digital projector.

Denis Litalien, Biddeford, Maine

I'm fifty-nine years old and lived in Biddeford all my life, so we would have been going to the Saco Drive-In when I was six to twelve years old, around 1960 to 1966 or thereabouts. "We" includes both my parents, my younger brother and three younger sisters. The memories are mostly fun. We also went to the Kennebunk Drive-In and the Portland Twin Drive-In in Scarborough during those years, but Saco was the favorite, as they had the best playground.

We had to be good during the week to "earn" the trip to the drive-in. It was a special treat for us to be taken there. Mom used to pack up sandwiches, whoopie pies and a jug of Kool-Aid or homemade root beer for the evening. We seldom went to the snack bar because of the expense.

We always got there early, and Dad parked close to the front so we could play on the swing set, monkey bars and other amusements while my parents watched us from the car. I remember one ride that went around like a miniature carousel that got you dizzy when you spun it too fast. My brother was especially good at getting the girls woozy!

Once it got dark enough and the previews started, we all got back to the car, a '56 Mercury, and claimed our places. The prime spot was lying on the rear deck above the backseat. You could lie down on top of the backseat against the rear window to watch the movie and usually fell asleep before the second feature. The next best spot was the middle of the front seat so you had an unobstructed view. Often Dad moved the car to the back line before the movie started so that we didn't have to crane our necks to see out the front window. Each parking row had a raised area to park the front wheels to tilt the car up at an angle for best viewing. Dad inched the car forward and back to adjust it so it was just right. Someone always left their headlights on at the start of the movie, which triggered a cacophony of horns to get the offender to shut them off so they wouldn't shine on the screen.

The speaker to hear the movie was attached to a wire on a pole, and it was hung on the window, and then the window was rolled up as tight as it would go.

Then we stuffed towels in the crack that was left to keep the mosquitoes out. Otherwise, Mom and Dad would blow cigarette smoke on us to discourage the mosquitoes from biting. We used to look forward to the man with the smoke machine coming around to discourage the mosquitoes. He had this contraption with a motor similar to today's leaf blowers attached to his back, and it blew this kerosene-smelling smoke throughout the parking area and seemed to help keep the mosquitoes at bay for a while. I can still recall the smell of that awful smoke to this day. At intermission, usually in between the two features, we were allowed to go to the bathroom and usually made the most of this trip out of the car to take a last ride on the swing set in the dark.

It was not unusual to see people drive off after the movie with the speaker still attached to the side of the car. It was also not unusual to see cars not start up after the movie and not move, as people often fell asleep in their cars and had to be awakened by the theater folks.

When we were teenagers and got our first cars, I can't tell you how many times I was able to convince my girlfriend to go the movies at the drive-in! I'm still married to the same girl, so it must have been a good thing for us to do! At that age, we always parked in the back. It was a great routine to go "parking" at the drive-in, then take a spin around the "Square" at Old Orchard Beach afterward before grabbing a couple of dogs at Rapid Ray's in Saco on the way home.

The drive-in brings some fun memories back. One memory in particular concerns the Portland Drive-In. My wife and two friends went to the Twin Drive-In in Scarborough in its later years and found we were the only car there

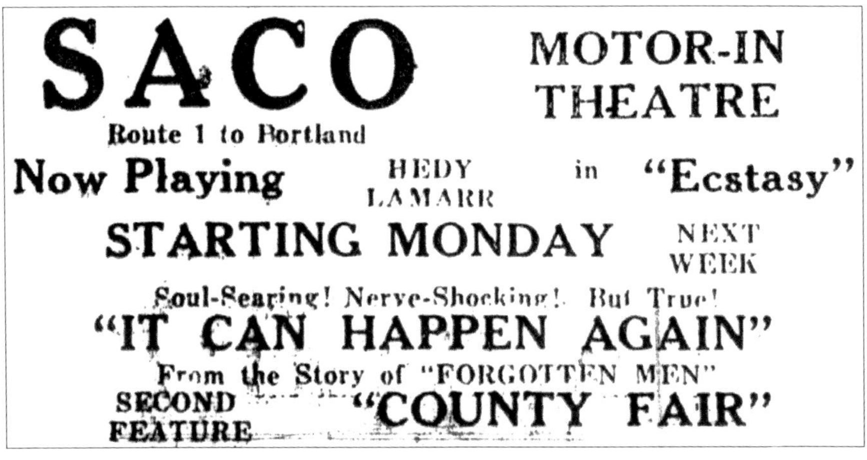

From the September 29, 1939 *Biddeford Daily Journal. McArthur Library Archives, Biddeford, Maine.*

as it started to snow. The person at the gate let us in and ran the movie for us exclusively. The person taking the tickets was the only one there and could not open the snack bar. At intermission, the movie did not start back up, so we went inside to check and found that he had fallen asleep before it was time to switch reels. After waking him up and letting him know that it was OK if he wanted to go home, as we had to keep running the windshield wipers to see the movie, he insisted that we finish it, and he put the second reel in and let us see the end.

Andrew Collins, Saco Drive-In Patron

I cannot tell you how happy I am the Saco Drive-In won a digital projector! I followed the story online and in the paper. The *Portland Press Herald* did a great job of covering the story, as did several others. I also read about it, I think, in the *Weekly Observer* I get in Sanford. I even remember as a kid that Sanford had a drive-in, and so did Acton. I don't think I ever went to the Sanford theater or the Acton theater, but I sort of remember them being around. Anyway, as an adult, I have taken my own children and my grandchildren to the Saco Drive-In. It's such a great place! You don't even feel like you're just off a major highway, either. You drive in, and it is just a big expanse of land with stalls and a concession stand. It feels like you're in your own little world with woods behind you and trees all around, plus the huge screen up front also surrounded by trees and bushes. It really feels you're in a giant-sized theater and you're tiny humans. My grandchildren always bring a football or their baseball gloves and play catch outside of the car before the film starts. My wife packs healthy snacks, since she doesn't want the kids to just eat fried foods or pizza, although they usually scoff at grapes but readily eat watermelon in exchange for a promise of ice cream. I would not trade those hours with my grandkids for the world, and I am so glad we can still attend summer films at the Saco Drive-In. It's always worth the drive.

Don Witham, Former Saco Drive-In Usher, Saco, Maine

I was born in Dunstan, Scarborough, and remember going to the drive-in when it first opened in 1939. I rode my bike with some friends from Scarborough to Saco, and the ticket man said I was too young for the film.

I was the head usher at the Saco Drive-In from 1946 through 1956. After World War II, I came home, and Mr. O'Neill, one of the owners (along with Boragine), asked me if I wanted to work at the drive-in. I said yes, and the Boragines were very nice people. Boragine was a happy-go-lucky man who really enjoyed having families and children at the drive-in. He really focused on the drive-in playing family movies, and he actually knew someone in the film business to get those first-run films. That summer in 1946, I met my wife, Jean. She was working as a ticket taker in the ticket booth at the drive-in, and we were married that fall…for forty-three years until her death.

In 1946 until about 1947, the drive-in had only one large speaker on top of the screen. It blared so loud people all the way down to Pine Point could hear the sound. People often complained about the noise from the theater, but no one ever actually did anything about it. When the individual speakers came along, I placed them on the cars and also fixed them whenever something was wrong. Sometimes I helped in the projection room with the two projectors that ran on carbons. They took up the entire room together. You had to wind the film reels and watch carefully to prevent a break in the film. When film broke, you used special cells to put it back together. Of course, [at] times, bugs came in and got stuck on the glass and skipped the film.

In the early days, the capacity was 125 cars. After the theater switched to individual car speakers, the space without the large speaker made room for more cars, bumping the drive-in up to 300 cars. A stockade fence was added after the loudspeaker was removed. About 1954, a new panoramic screen was installed. In the late 1940s, the drive-in sold hot dogs from the ticket booth, and you didn't have to buy a ticket to buy a hot dog Then, later, there were two concession stands, one beside the projection room and one to the far right upon entering the theater. Both stands sold hot dogs, ice cream, hamburgers, soda and coffee. The playground was off to the right and had slides and swings for the kids.

We had many popular films at the Saco Drive-In back in the '40s and '50s. I remember we had the *Greatest Show on Earth* play in 1956 or 1957 from dusk until dawn. The drive-in was packed. This movie came out in about '52 with Charlton Heston, Jimmy Stewart and Betty Hutton. Everyone loved it. We also had Cecil A. Moore, also known as "Mush" Moore, come and talk about his adventures running a dog sled from Lewiston to Alaska. Many people enjoyed the Saco Drive-In in those days.

No traffic yet. *Courtesy of James Leary.*

Ben Stone, Saco Drive-In Patron, New York

I grew up on the West Coast. We had a drive-in theater nearby that we used to go to all the time. We loved it. I saw some of the best movies there, and it's one of the few times I can remember having a double feature for the price of one ticket. Sadly, like most drive-ins, it closed down. I always missed going to the drive-in theater. My in-laws have a house in Old Orchard Beach, so when I moved to New York, my wife and I [would] always go to the Saco Drive-In. We love it so much we went during our honeymoon. We come up to Maine multiple times during the summer, and now that we are expecting our first addition to our family (twins!), we plan on taking them to enjoy the experience of the drive-in theater. I am deeply saddened to learn there is a need for a "save the drive-in." I truly hope it is saved and we can pass on one of my favorite American pastimes—the drive-in movie.

Amanda, Saco Drive-In Patron, Boston, Massachusetts

The Saco Drive-In is by far one of my favorite parts about going on vacation in Maine. There are so few around, and the Saco Drive-In is a gem. Camping out on my mom's rooftop when I was a kid to watch the drive-in movies under the stars is by far one of my favorite memories. I'm twenty-four now and still look forward to visiting the Saco Drive-In whenever I vacation in Maine. I get that warm feeling of nostalgia every time I go to the Saco Drive-In. It's a place that reminds me of childhood and more.

Fran Beaulieu, Saco Drive-In Patron

I remember going to my first drive-in to watch *ET*. It was the best time. My brother and I wore our PJs and brought pillows. My mom and aunt spoiled us with popcorn and snacks. Many years later, I have shared this experience with my kids. We have watched movies at the Saco Drive-In at least once each summer, but we make it an adventure. We bring chairs, bug spray, pillows and blankets to enjoy movies in the great outdoors! I can only hope that there are drive-ins around for my kids to share the experience with their own kids.

Richard Julio, Former Projectionist, Saco Drive-In, Portland, Maine

I have [run] the projector at the Saco Drive-In for many, many years. I have done a variety of jobs in my life, including booking rock bands and acts at the original Genos in Portland. I actually started working with movie projectors at indoor movie theaters, often running multiple projectors in different sections of the theater. I thought running film was pretty fun and eventually was approached to assist with getting the Saco Drive-In theater up and running. This was in the '80s, I think. The Saco Drive-In's projector, the one they are replacing with the digital projector, isn't actually the original projector. I have no idea what happened to that one. Maybe it died or it was taken by the previous manager, I don't know. It's also really cold here in the winter, so maybe that caused some sort of internal damage. Something happened to that one. I am fairly certain the theater had two projectors, as in the 1950s and 1960s, you often ran two projectors to run two-hour films.

So the Saco Drive-In didn't have a projector—or didn't have a working projector at any rate—so the owners bought a drive-in projector from the drive-in that used to be in Camden, Maine. They brought it down to Saco, and I helped clean it out and set it up, making sure it was ready to run film. I ran film with a friend for many years, from the 1980s through 2013. I don't know what's going to happen now that we have digital. I would imagine that there won't be any setup time like there is for the film projection system. I used to have to set the wheels and prep them for the show and then just sit and watch them during the movie to make sure nothing broke or had issues. Then, during intermission, I would change the film reels and repeat the same process I did for the first film. After you set up the projector, there really isn't much else to do. I often bring crossword puzzles to do during the show.

However, I have heard some interesting stories during my time here, and this is one of them. During the summer of 1967, a Canadian judge came to the drive-in in his brand-new 1967 Oldsmobile Tornado. Projectionist Hugh L. Howard (1966–1970) was watching the credits going by at the end of the movie when he saw headlights coming his way from over the ramps. He dove out of the way just as the car crashed through the fence and into the projection booth at full throttle! The car ruined the number one projector and sound amplifiers and of course caused major building damage. No one was hurt, and the projectionist commented that he knew the movie was bad but didn't think it warranted wrecking the projection booth! One of many interesting stories and happenings at the Saco Drive-In. This place has been a very interesting place to work, especially observing the changes in film, managers and patrons over the years.

Michael Petit, Saco, Maine

Back in the late '40s, my mom, dad and we three kids (under five) went to the SDI every week—every time new movies came to town. We lived in a small house at the site of what is now the Chevy dealership, and we were about a mile from the drive-in. It was great. Virtually every movie was appropriate for us kids. When not, we usually got bored and fell asleep. Mom brought popcorn, Kool-Aid and other treats. It was great.

The entrance, circa 2002. *Courtesy of James Leary.*

N. Simpson, Boston, Massachusetts

I grew up in Brookline, Massachusetts, but my family held several family reunions in Maine during the 1950s and 1960s. I don't remember the mid-1950s events very well, but I have seen the photographs. My aunt had a summer cottage in Camp Ellis, and we often gathered there. We held the actual reunion on the beach and used Ferry Beach a few times, as there was more space. After the barbecue and the food [were] eaten, we had all chatted and caught up all day, the whole family went to the drive-in. I think my parents and my aunts and uncles used this as a reward for us kids for being well behaved.

I remember cheek-pinching great-aunts and great-uncles with their Manhattans sitting out on the lawn at the house in Camp Ellis. The best part was the sun went down and we'd pile into cars to go to the drive-in. My cousins and I played on the playground behind a white building—I think it was the concession stand. But I think there could have been two concession stands—or I am confusing it with another drive-in in Massachusetts? Either way, we always played on the playground until nearly show time. Dad and my uncles would fetch us ice cream from the stand. We *had* to eat the ice cream outside of the car. That was the one rule: no food in the car. We saw

The Great Locomotive Chase, *Old Yeller* and *The Swiss Family Robinson.* I remember seeing horror films listed on the sign, but we were never allowed to see them. I hadn't thought about those memories in years, not until I saw the Saco Drive-In on the news for winning a digital projector. I had assumed that theater closed years ago, when all the other ones did. Glad to see a piece of my childhood is still open for others to enjoy.

Joseph Allen, New Hampshire

My sister sent me an e-mail with a link to the Saco Drive-In Facebook page. When we were kids, our parents used to take us to the Saco Drive-In on our way up to Rockland. When I saw they were in a contest to win a digital projector, I thought, "Good for them. They deserve it for being open for so many years." I can only imagine in seventy-four years the number of families, local Mainers and out-of-state guests, that theater has entertained. I also didn't realize that there were still so many drive-in theaters left, thanks to Honda's website. At that time in 2013, only about three hundred theaters. Frankly, I thought it was a lot less. It's a shame Hollywood won't continue on with the film projector. I think part of the whole drive-in experience is the sound the projector makes and hearing the film on the reel. Nothing can replace that sound. Even when you're watching a film, you can hear it when your windows are down. I suppose that the digital projector will be a clearer picture and all, like at the regular theater, but there is something to that sound.

As kids, we all enjoyed that visit. We often stayed in Scarborough on Route 1. We never did stay at the Cascades; it was always listed as No Vacancy every time we drove by. I would have also liked to have stayed there before it closed and was torn down. But I'm very glad the Saco Drive-In has a digital projector and can continue its business. Maine's summer is one of the best times of year—why waste it being in an indoor theater when you have the beautiful Maine woods plus the smell of the ocean? Who knows, perhaps someone will put a soundtrack on that makes the film sound play on the digital projector or use the old countdown till show time. Either way, the Saco Drive-In will remain a place for families.

Bobbi-Jo Levessque, Saco Drive-In Patron

I'm a faithful patron of the Saco Drive-In's movies. I've brought friends with me and converted friends into going to the drive-in, specifically during the summer, and staying out of the theaters both because of the amazing atmosphere and fun but also to support a local business. I've also gone by myself, just me and my dog; we've watched movies and eaten popcorn and the great nachos from the concession stand. One specific memory that I hold dear to me isn't a recent memory at all; it's from when I was a kid. My parents took me to the drive-in. We set up the backseat of the car like a bedroom, with blankets and pillows, and we went in our pajamas. I ate popcorn, candy, drank soda and felt all grown up watching *Grease* for the first time. We sang and danced, and I remember the box speaker my dad put in the window and the scratchy sounds that came from it, the mosquito burner on the dashboard and the other cars around us. I remember watching my parents hold hands while watching the movies. I'll never forget that experience and really want to have more families share these types of memories with their kids and their kids' kids.

Paula Collins, Shrewsbury, Massachusetts

My family loves the drive-in. My kids grew up with a drive-in less than a mile from our house, and when it closed, my eldest was devastated. We came to visit grandparents in [Old Orchard Beach] and found the Saco Drive-In. We go every time we are in Maine—rain or shine! It is sad that they are closing all over the country. Please don't let this American tradition go! There is nothing better than a lawn chair and fresh air and plenty of room to dance to the soundtrack. My most recent memory was taking my eldest and his buddy to see a movie. As film majors, that is always a trip, but on this night, the drive-in was cleaning out the strips of film from the trailers. These two were like kids in a candy store! They were up for hours checking out the mini films and trying to figure out what to do with them.

"Snack Bar Lights." *Courtesy Charlie Widdis Photography©.*

Ms. Tripp, Saco, Maine

I worked at the Cascades restaurant while I was in my late teens during the summers in the 1950s. I worked a variety of shifts, sometimes closing one evening and opening for breakfast the next morning. Cascades had dormitories for servers, particularly in that situation. I had several friends who did not live very far from the Cascades Inn or the Saco Drive-In, but when you worked that back-to-back closing-then-opening shift, even going three miles that early in the morning seemed like quite a bike ride, or a walk or sometimes a car ride. After closing up in the evening, a group of us would climb through the shrubs and watch films at the Saco Drive-In without actually going into the drive-in. We couldn't hear the movie very clearly, but it was free and a great way to blow off steam after work.

Henry Owen, Future Saco Drive-In Patron

I have never actually been inside of the Saco Drive-In, but I drive past it regularly. I had gone to a drive-in theater once as a child, but it was a very

"Dusk at the Drive-In." *Courtesy Charlie Widdis Photography*©.

long time ago. I followed all the stories about the theater and joined their Facebook page to watch the contest. I voted and reposted. I know this probably sounds strange, but I really wanted to save the drive-in. After reading about Ry Russell, Justin Chenette and Camille Smalley's work at the theater and how hard they were committed, I felt compelled. I've always seen the drive-in while traveling Route 1, and I have often thought to myself, "I should go there." I never realized that those future thoughts and plans could be cut off by Hollywood not producing film. I realized that I haven't really explored all my town has to offer; instead, I treated Saco more like a bedroom community. I come home, and I usually go to Portland for my free time. However, Saco *does* have a lot to offer. I didn't give this theater much of a second thought until I saw the *Courier* article about drive-in theaters going dark. The community also rallied to save the Saco Central Fire Station and stepped up again to save the Saco Drive-In. I will be going to see a film at the Saco Drive-In this summer. It's something that should be celebrated for sure.

Mandy Pilon, Saco, Maine

I went to the Saco Drive-In one evening with some friends. It was a nice summer evening and great weather to see a movie. The Saco Drive-In still has the poles where the in-car speakers hung before they were placed on the car. I backed up to leave and *SCRAPE!* I hit the pole with the car. I got out of the car, and sure enough, there was a good scratch on the side of my parents' car. It's a laugh now, but I was pretty nervous about it then. The Saco Drive-In was part of my teenage years growing up in Saco.

Jessica Layne, Richmond, Virginia

Every summer, my family drove up from Richmond, Virginia, to Bar Harbor, Maine. We often stopped in several towns along the way, one of which was Saco. It was a nice stopping point with beaches and spending an afternoon in Old Orchard Beach. We always made a point to stop at the Saco Drive-In. For our family, we really enjoyed lying in the back of the SUV and smelling the sweet summer air. We have enjoyed films at the Saco Drive-In since the late 1990s and look forward to continuing the tradition every year.

Doug Scamman, Maine

My wife and I went on one of our first dates at the Saco Drive-In, back in the 1970s. I remember buying her soda and popcorn at the concession stand while I opted for a slice of pizza. We watched the first film, which was something about demons or possession, I can't really remember now. I do remember not paying that much attention to the second film, and it really didn't matter. The drive-in has a special memory for me, my wife and many other people. So many people have seen films at that theater; it's hard to imagine anyone not enjoying themselves. Saco is very lucky.

Anatole Therriault, Biddeford, Maine

For my family in the 1960s, the Saco Drive-In was a treat. We took the entire family to see films from the time the theater opened in April or May until it closed in September or October and, one year, November. The kids enjoyed hot dogs and pizza at the snack bar. I was glad to be out of the house with my wife. Before the first film and often during intermission, the kids played on the playground by the snack bar. Most often, the backseat was asleep during the second film, and my wife and I would carry the children in to bed. It was an inexpensive outing for the family and always an enjoyable, laid-back experience.

Elizabeth West, Saco, Maine

Oh, the Saco Drive-In! I remember my husband and I taking our daughter to the drive-in. We summered at Camp Ellis and visited the drive-in after spending the day swimming at the cottage. I packed up snacks in a cooler and brought it with us. My husband often bought ice cream from the concession stand at intermission, and we ate dinner at the picnic tables. Of course, the mosquitoes could be pretty bad out there off Route 1, but not too much worse than anyplace else in Maine during the summer. It was funny when a bug would get stuck on the film reel, but that does not happen much anymore with digital film. The drive-in offered more privacy than the Mutual Theater in downtown Saco and was much cheaper. It was a lovely time with my family, and I cherish the memories.

Sarah Conner, Saco, Maine

Drive-ins have a special place in my heart! We used to take our children to the drive-in on Friday and Saturday nights in their pajamas. The kids loved it; they enjoyed putting their pajamas on early and getting ready to head out to the drive-in. We treated them to candy and ice cream before intermission. My husband and I enjoyed the second film while the kids slept—it was very nice to have some adult time while knowing the children are taken care of. We never had a babysitter very often, and this allowed us to have the best of

A summer evening at the Saco Drive-In. *Courtesy of James Leary.*

both worlds. After the second movie, we drove home, and the children went straight to bed. It really was a family place!

Jennifer Friedland, Saco, Maine

The Saco Drive-In. I remember visiting the theater with my friends when we were in high school in the '60s. Of course, borrowing one of our parents' cars, sneaking a couple friends in the backseat, it was the best. Sometimes, we would meet up with the boys in the parking lot and switch cars. Lots of things our parents wouldn't want to know about happened at the drive-in, but it was all a part of growing up.

Francis Cote, Arundel, Maine

I remember when the Saco Drive-In had two concession stands—the current stand, which was considered the main stand, I suppose, and then another one off to the side. As a child, I always had to visit both of them, one to get a hot dog and the other to get an ice cream. There was something about having two stands that really made the experience great. I would always leave my parents just as the credits started to roll and raced to the stand on the right side of the theater to beat the crowd. There was always a group of kids waiting.

Robert Johnson, South Portland, Maine

I never really gave drive-in theaters much thought as a place to go while on vacation. Growing up in South Carolina, I don't remember having a drive-in within close driving distance. My parents had mentioned them when talking about things they did in their childhood, but I never considered it. I lived in South Carolina until I was a teenager and moved to Maine with a friend. I was bored, and it sounded like a good idea in the 1960s. So we drove up Route 1 from South Carolina and first bummed around Portland. It was beautiful that summer; however, reality set in, and we needed to get real jobs. I ended up working in Scarborough for a local grocer. There, I saw the Portland Twin Drive-In off Route 1 and, while visiting a girl I met in Saco, passed the Saco Drive-In, also off of Route 1. It was late August, and we were hanging out at the beach in Camp Ellis with a few other kids. The sun started to set, and she suggested we head to the Saco Drive-In. They were playing a double feature of one of those Vincent Price films, the really gory ones. Perhaps it was something about body snatchers or aliens—I think I remember aliens. Then again, a lot of movies were like that at the drive-in. I also ended up seeing that Romero zombie film, *Night of the Living Dead*, sometime at the drive-in also. Anyway, so we watched the gory movie, which was great, as I really liked the girl and we were able to cuddle up, especially during the scary parts, in the car.

The drive-in was a completely different experience than any other theater. Being outside, as well as in the dark car, was great. It was an experience unlike any other. After I married—not the same girl as at the drive-in, but another lovely girl—and had some children, we bought a house in Maine. I now take my grandchildren and wife to the drive-in during the summer. We all enjoy piling in the car, and this has as much nostalgia for me as it does for my wife, as she grew up frequenting the drive-in as well. I enjoyed watching the kids have fun at the theater, eating pizza, ice cream and playing catch before the film starts. I hope they enjoy our time together as much as I do. The drive-in is a special place from my later adulthood, and I hope it will be a special place in my grandchildren's hearts.

Mary Sheppard, North Andover, Massachusetts

My family used to spend summers up in Old Orchard Beach and sometimes in Ocean Park. We often would rent a small cottage a few blocks away from the pier. This was in the 1950s, when renting cottages was less expensive than it is today. We stayed usually down closer to the water, but one time, my father wanted to stay in one of the cottages at Cascades. We only did that one time, though, as he preferred to only be a short walk from the beach as opposed to having to drive down to the beach and the pier. That made it a little more difficult, and there was not very much parking. Plus, Father did not like having sandy feet inside his Plymouth, so it was easier to rent a cottage closer to the water.

We spent a week or two down in Old Orchard, usually. Some years, it was a week; some years, it was two weeks. I guess it depended on how much money we had for vacations at that time. I had two brothers and a sister, so it couldn't have been easy for my parents to afford vacations. We stayed at a cottage because mother could still cook meals like she would at home, which was often cheaper. Of course, we did have snacks at the pier. We would walk down to the pier and walk the length of it. Sometimes big acts played. I remember Mother and Father discussing how Glenn Miller came to the pier and played music. They danced the jitterbug to "In the Mood" all night.

On the drive to Old Orchard, we always took Route 1. The road by the water was always better and more recreational than any other stretch of road. My parents often stopped to snap photographs, and we squished on the hood of the car. We always passed the Saco Drive-In, with its big marquee. Every vacation, we spent one evening at the drive-in. Mother brought a basket of snacks from home, and we piled into the car. My brothers always enjoyed when mosquitoes would get stuck on the screen and the film would blur. I thought it was disgusting. I also did not care for the mosquitoes that came in the windows when you rolled them down. But that could not be helped, seeing as it was Maine and the summertime.

I have fond memories of enjoying a film, elbowing my brothers and sister and just having a good time in Old Orchard and Saco.

Lynette Wheeler, Saco, Maine

We filled up our old Chevy truck with hay and brought a bunch of blankets and pillows. At first, I was appalled at my husband by doing that! But in the end, he won…it was so comfortable. So much so, my two daughters and I passed out before the movie was done! Only the boys made it through both films without falling asleep.

Lynette Wheeler's family enjoying a cozy summer night at the Saco Drive-In. *Courtesy of Lynette Wheeler.*

Jennifer Stiles, Portsmouth, New Hampshire

Drive-ins are essential to keeping the good old days of movie watching alive. My husband and I really enjoy the experience and the atmosphere. We can't wait to go again this summer, and it would be so sad if it were to end. Thanks for giving us something to look forward to on a Saturday night in summer!

Karen Thompson, Saco Drive-In Patron

My grandparents live in Bath, Maine, and I go see them every summer I can. Usually, myself and a few friends drive up to Brunswick and stay with them at their house for a few days. They have a water view and a large, beautiful home, so it's a real treat to stay with them. My friends and I usually gather at my house and catch a movie at the Saco Drive-In the evening before we leave since we typically leave around noon. The group of us have been seeing movies at the drive-in for quite a while now and almost always bring a radio with us. I prefer the portable radio, as we don't have to use the car radio to tune into the station and worry about the battery in the car. This time, of course, the radio gets forgotten.

We get to the drive-in, we park and then hit up the snack bar for some French fries, chicken strips, ice cream and, of course, popcorn. After settling back in, I ask for the radio and am told no one grabbed it, but "that's okay, we can just use the car radio and it will be just fine." So we watched the first movie, then got some more ice cream and then watched the second film. I pushed the keys in the off position as we cleaned up the car and waited for our turn to leave. I go to turn the car on and nothing comes on. The battery was completely dead. How it died in that ten minutes of time, I have no idea. So now all the cars around us have gone, and we're still sitting there. Luckily, the staff at the Saco Drive-In are awesome, and they have a battery charger like AAA does, and they'll come around and jump the cars that are left behind. That particular night, we were one of five cars! *Five!* I felt bad so many other people had the same issue but relieved. We got the car started and left. I will never forget that. I kept singing John Travolta's line from *Grease*: "Stranded at the drive-in…"

Frank Barnako, Wiscasset, Maine, and Great Falls, Virginia

Last summer, I chose the Saco Drive-In for a photography project. I was aware the studios were planning to curtail 35mm distribution, and I wanted to have a record of drive-ins before they disappeared. I met Ry Russell, and I explained that I'd done a project about Maine diners two years earlier because I like diners and saw that they are gradually closing. I knew the same story was being written about drive-ins. As a kid, I enjoyed diners and drive-ins.

Ry welcomed me, introduced me to the snack bar people and the projectionist and let me wander around several evenings. I struck up conversations with folks in their cars, on their lawn chairs and on the playground. Folks on a date in their pickup, groups of families getting together, older couples just out for the evening.

Quickly, I realized drive-ins are different than diners. You don't remember the design or layout or architecture of a drive-in. It's just a big field with a concrete building, and when it gets dark, there are lots of bugs.

What you do remember is what you did there. You remember being a little girl with your grandmother indulging you on summer evenings in New Jersey as she sits through a double creature-feature while you gorge on soda and popcorn. (This is my wife's memory.) You remember necking with a date. (My memory.) And you remember playing games with your friends and families sharing a good time.

Laurie-Jean Gombar, Saco Drive-In Patron

Thank you, Saco Drive-In! We were able to go to a movie—actually lots of them that summer—with an infant. Our son is now eight years old with a five-year-old sister. We enjoy bringing both kids with us to the Saco Drive-In theater. Everyone enjoys it!

Ted Richards, Saco Drive-In Patron

You can't trust a person who doesn't like the Saco Drive-In! This theater has been a permanent piece of Saco for quite a long time and has been entertaining crowds of families for ages. I often take Route 1 to Portland,

Laurie Gombar and her infant at the Saco Drive-In. *Courtesy of Laurie Jean Gombar.*

and in the summer, there are always cars backed up, starting at about 5:30 to 6:00 p.m., just waiting to get into the Saco Drive-In. It's really great to see a local Saco business still trucking after so many years. Drive-ins really represent that auto age in America and freedom. The ability to get in your car and just go and enjoy a film. I went to the drive-in as a teenager; it was a great place to take a date. I am sure kids still do that, but it's a great place to take a family, too—but I suppose that's always been the case. Who doesn't love a film outside? I remember as a kid we used to burn candles or pic wire to keep away the mosquitoes. That isn't allowed now, which makes sense. It's Maine—you have to have something to keep away those bugs! Still, the drive-in, bugs or no, is the best way to watch a movie in Vacationland!

Alexis Moody, Scarborough, Maine

There is nothing like packing up a cooler, bringing some blankets, the comfortable lawn chairs with the cup holders and watching a movie at the Saco Drive-In. For my family, this is something that happens every summer and multiple times per season. Money is tight for us and has been for a while, but thanks to the great prices at the Saco Drive-In, we can take all three kids out to enjoy two movies for the matinee prices of two adult tickets at a regular

From the October 17, 1939 *Biddeford Daily Journal. McArthur Library Archives, Biddeford, Maine.*

movie theater, not counting food. I don't know how the Saco Drive-In is able to do this, but I am grateful. Our family enjoys the time outdoors and with a great film together. Last season, we went and saw *Monsters University*, and the entire drive-in was packed. I think they sold out that weekend. I can't recall the second film, but there were so many families, laughter and smiles. Thanks, Saco Drive-In!

Heather Lund, Saco Drive-In Patron

The Saco Drive-In has meant so much to our family. Though we started late in the game, the summer of 2010, it was during a time in our family's life where finances had become almost unbearable. Truth be told, the Saco Drive-In saved our family during that time. To spend those warm nights, close together, in laughter and total enjoyment, helped us to give our children a smile each week and for my husband and I to bond despite the stress and struggle we were under. The kids were able to bring friends along as well at times, and what a gift the Saco Drive-In gives kids and teens alike. To share a memory, a rooftop viewing, on a warm summer night with a friend. In fact, it was that year that our youngest child was born, and he spent one night every weekend there with us his first summer, asleep in his car seat with mosquito netting over the top. We continue to make a stop at the Saco Drive-In each week, every summer. For some, it's nostalgia; for us, it's a place where the worries of life are left at the gate, and we sink back into a comfortable place, surrounded by our children, and just enjoy ourselves. The drive-in is the only place we spend our money for current films because of the social and family-friendly/bonding aspect. We can't let this disappear.

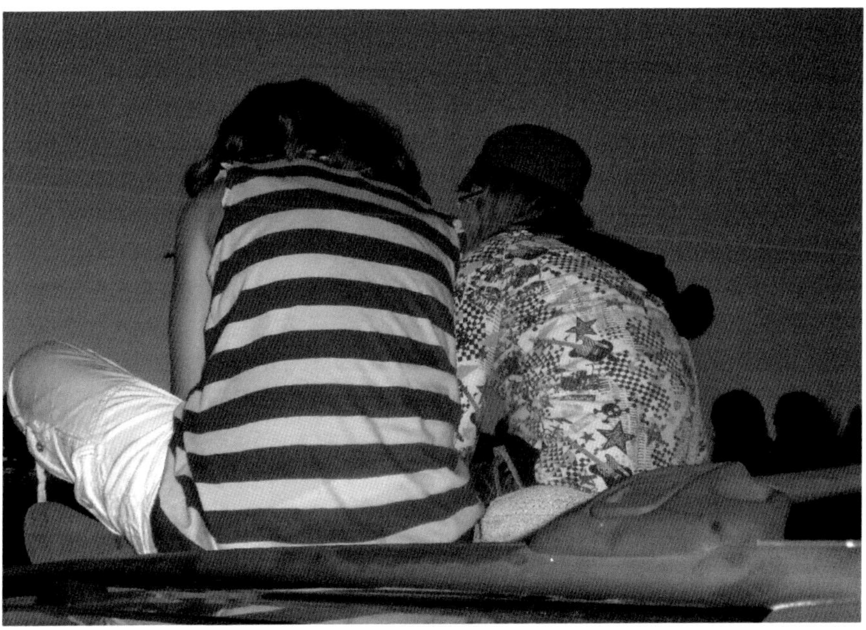

Family night out. *Courtesy of Heather Lund.*

The Potter Family, Waterville, Maine

Every story I have regarding the Saco Drive-In is a great one. My family and I have never had a bad experience even once in all the years we've been going. We now live in Waterville and still make the ride down for the best double features in New England. If I had the capital, I'd buy the place and never miss a night—but unfortunately, I don't, so my family will do what it always has and continue supporting the experience by attending as often as we can and pray the Saco Drive-In, a "true piece of Americana," never closes its gates!

Lisamarie Ward, Saco Drive-In Patron

My girlfriend and I had our first date at the Saco Drive-In. We have been together for almost eight years now. We are very excited that Maine has passed the same-sex marriage law—now we can be wed! We are considering using the Saco Drive-In as a location considering it was where we had our first date. This place has special memories for us and always will!

Ray Gaudette, Biddeford Historical Society, Biddeford, Maine

The drive-in is a great invention. Before I was married, I used to go to the drive-in with my friends. They would try to decide who should ride in the trunk so the admission was less—of course, being the smallest, they always wanted me to ride in the trunk, but I said absolutely not. We visited all the drive-ins—Biddeford, Sanford, Kennebunk—it just depended on who had the best movies playing at the time. Sometimes it was Sanford, sometimes Saco, sometimes Kennebunk; it really varied, but they all had double features. I remember getting out of the car and seeing who else was at the drive-in before the film started. After starting a family, my wife and I often brought the children to the drive-in. It was very easy to bring them already dressed in their pajamas. They usually fell asleep before the second film, and we carried them in the house after arriving home. The drive-in was, and still is, a great place for families to visit.

Excited for an evening at the Saco Drive-In. *Courtesy of the Perry family.*

Snack sharing at the Saco Drive-In. *Courtesy of the Perry family.*

Marilyn Brenner, Massachusetts and Maine

As a young girl, my family traveled up and down Route 1 on vacation. This was in the later 1950s and probably into the 1960s—it all runs together a bit now. I do remember driving through Maine in the family's Ford Fairlane. There were many drive-ins along the roadway at that time, including one in Kittery or York, Kennebunk, Saco, Scarborough and perhaps one in Portland as well, but I can't remember. We visited quite a few when we stayed in different places. Saco and Kennebunk often played the same movies at the same time—I guess they were able to get the same ones. My dad would pick up a newspaper at a diner and see what the day's events would be. Almost every vacation, we went to a drive-in at least one time. I remember the Saco Drive-In, mostly because of the water fountain at the front. My mother thought it was strange that there were two polar bears along with a deer. I didn't think anything of it. I liked to eat dinner at the picnic tables by the fountain and watch the cars pull into the theater. I am happy this sweet, family place was saved for future generations by the actions of the people in Saco. Way to go, Saco.

Heidi Young, Saco Drive-In Patron

My family and I love the Saco Drive-In. We come several times during the summer. We live on a tight income, so it's such a treat to be able to watch two movies. Our son's girlfriend had never been to a drive-in until this past summer when we went on a double date with them. It's an absolutely remarkable place that we want to be able to bring our grandson [to] this summer and many summers to come.

Matthew Gilbert, Saco, Maine

The Saco Drive-In is certainly a landmark on Route 1. Anyone in the last seventy or so years who has lived in the area, even if they have never been to the actual theater, knows what the Saco Drive-In is and about where it is. The theater has had a real revival in the last fifteen or so years. I remember in the 1980s when there were several questionable films on the marquee

First time at the drive-in! *Courtesy of Heidi Young.*

and no one really discussed the theater in a positive way. Or if the theater was mentioned, conversations would start with: "Remember when it was a family place?" But in the 1990s, the theater acquired better films. They still showed more R films, but they tried to incorporate as many family films as possible. Now, the drive-in is easily the best place to take the family for fifteen dollars. You can even bring your own snacks and only pay fifteen dollars to get in. I followed the contest for the digital projector and was very happy to see the community rally behind the drive-in. The staff at the theater really worked hard and fought tooth and nail for their theater in their community. I am proud to say the Saco Drive-In has and will stand the test of time. Granted, some of the original signage is missing, but the theater still looks sharp for being the second-oldest still functional drive-in theater in America. How great is that? Saco, with two hundred years of history, also gets to boast having one of the oldest drive-in theaters in the country. It is a real genuine and historically important place.

Eric and Wendy Brown, Old Orchard Beach, Maine

When my husband and I met in 1994, we were both enlisted soldiers in the U.S. Army and stationed in Germany. Perhaps not love at first sight, but certainly we figured out pretty quickly that we wanted to spend the rest of our lives together. Unfortunately, before we could make it official, the army decided that he needed to move to Kansas—and so he did. Undeterred, we planned our wedding over the phone, long-distance, me in Germany and him in Kansas. In May 1995, he drove from Kansas to Maine, and I flew from Germany to Maine. We were united in marriage at a sunrise ceremony in Biddeford Pool and then spent the next few days at the Samoset Resort. The night before we had to leave Maine for an uncertain future that would include a period of separation (and we had no idea how long that would be) when he reported back to Kansas and I reported back to Germany, we went to our first movie as husband and wife. It was at the Saco Drive-In theater, and one of the two films that night was the award-winning *Legends of the Fall* with Brad Pitt.

In 1997, my husband and I were both honorably discharged from our enlistments. We moved to Maine and bought a house—two miles from the Saco Drive-In. Fifteen years and three children later, we are thrilled to share the drive-in experience with our daughters and spend at least one evening every year, usually at the beginning of the season, at the drive-in. The Saco Drive-In has played a background role in our lives for as long as we've been married. We love going there for so many reasons, the least of which is just the sheer enjoyment of watching a movie in an outdoor theater. I can't imagine Route 1 in Saco, Maine, without the drive-in. With many thanks for all of our fun moviegoing experiences.

Annie Phillips, Glen Cove, New York

I've been taking the kids to Maine for a week or two for several years now. This past summer, we went to the Saco Drive-In for the first time. It brought back great childhood memories of going to the drive-in as a kid, and my kids had a blast. The night, we went just after a storm and power outage.

Sharing drive-in nostalgia with a new generation. *Courtesy of Annie Phillips.*

Summer showers bring dusky rainbows. *Courtesy of Annie Phillips.*

Michele Alexander and Evangeline, Saco Drive-In Patrons

We love the drive-in! The first time we went, we saw *Dolphin Tale*, and then we went to Clearwater, Florida, and met Winter, the star of the movie! It was a wonderful experience that we look forward to repeating.

Karen St. Pierre, Saco Drive-In Patron

After leaving a very bad marriage, I moved home. I love Maine so much. This was the only place I wanted to raise my two boys. After eighteen years of marriage, my funds just are not the same anymore. Before this, I could have taken my boys to the theater at least six or seven times a year. Now I am lucky if we get to come twice a year, and much thanks to the Saco Drive-In for making that possible. With the low cost of tickets at the Saco Drive-In, I can come to the theater at two-thirds the cost of an indoor theater. It is even worse if my boyfriend and I want to bring all of our kids, because he has three and I have two, so that makes us a very huge party. If we went to the regular movie theater, it would be fifty dollars just for tickets, never mind drinks and popcorn for everyone. I can remember coming to the drive-in when I was a kid and enjoy bringing my boys here now.

McKegg Collins, Saco Drive-In Patron

One of my favorite memories of the Saco Drive-In was when I brought a good friend of mine to the theater. We are both film majors at school and love drive-ins. After the first movie was over, there was an announcement that they were selling trailer prints. We got super excited and ran over there. I walked away with three prints, one of which was *Where the Wild Things Are*, an important movie to me. We walked out happy film nerds, and I plan to keep those forever. I don't want this place to close. It literally breaks my heart when great drive-ins close. It's a piece of Americana I think should be protected and preserved.

Melanie, Jeff, Max and Robbie Kyer, York, Maine

I am originally from Maine, but I have been living out of state for the past fifteen years. Then last year, I was lucky enough to find my dream job teaching in York. My husband quit his job, and we left the rat race of the D.C. suburbs and came to small-town life in rural Maine. With two boys, aged three and six, we rarely get the chance to go to the movies since it usually means not only expensive prices but also an expensive sitter bill. I

Almost show time! *Courtesy of Melanie Kyer.*

Snacking in the SUV. *Courtesy of Melanie Kyer.*

was thrilled to learn that there were still drive-ins around, particularly one relatively close to us! We went several times last summer, and the boys just loved it. Of course, they were generally both asleep by the time the movies started, but that didn't matter. They still beg us to go to the drive-in because that means they get to sit in the back of the SUV, eat a picnic, have popcorn, run around in the big parking lot, blow bubbles and stay up way past their bedtime. And Mom and Dad get to see the latest movies without going broke! It's a magical throwback to a simpler time that definitely still has a place in our lives. I can't wait for you to open up again this season! Long live the Saco Drive-In!

Peter Morelli, City of Saco Planning and Economic Development, Portland, Maine

In 1972, there was a double-date double feature with the movie *Ben* and a Scandinavian police movie. The movies were terrible, but I really liked the girl. *Ben* was about a boy protected by the rat named Ben and was a sequel to the previous year's *Willard*. The only good thing about the movies was the Michael Jackson theme "I've got a friend in Ben"—even if it is about a rat. By the way, I talked to the girl (now fifty-nine) recently after several decades, and she doesn't remember any of it!

Laura Snyder, Saco Drive-In Patron

The more things change, the more they stay the same! I went to the Saco Drive-In as a child with my family, and I bring my own family to the drive-in now. I distinctly remember going as a child, and we would bring snacks with us to eat in the car. Plenty of times, I fell asleep before the end of the second film and would be awakened when my father carried me up to bed. There was one time, I think it was something like 1963 or 1965, and I was playing on the playground that was underneath the screen. It was a chilly summer evening; it had been a wet week. I had on a light waterproof jacket at my mother's insistence. The trailers began, and I dashed back to the car with my sister. We ate and watched two films plus a cartoon—I think it was a Disney cartoon of some sort. The next day, I go to grab my rain jacket, and it's nowhere to be found. It was not in the car or the mudroom. It was fairly new, and my parents were disappointed that I had left it at the theater. My mother phoned the theater and left a message about the missing jacket. Later that evening, after dinner, we received a phone call that someone had found the jacket and they would keep it at the ticket booth for us. Thanks to the great staff, I got my jacket back. My parents could not have afforded a new one at that time. I'm proud to say that when I go with my family to the Saco Drive-In, the staff is very friendly and kind. It's a wonderful experience, and I am very pleased we can continue to enjoy films at the Saco Drive-In.

Constance Downs, Saco Drive-In Patron

Cuddled up and ready for the movie. *Courtesy of Shirley Markland.*

I went to the Saco Drive-In with my boyfriend quite often in the early 1970s. My mother thought I was going with a group of girlfriends, but she never knew that I actually just met up with my boyfriend at the drive-in and watched the films with him. I am sure she would be horrified to know that now. I remember seeing films like *Night of the Living Dead*, *House on Haunted Hill*, *Last House on the Left* and other incredibly gory films. Most people I knew who went to the drive-in enjoyed those films, too—well, when they were paying attention to the films. By then, there were not as many families at the theater as there had been when I was a child. By then, it was more those of us teenagers who had newfound freedom with the car. I think the drive-in gave us that freedom to just be and experience life on our own.

Camille M. Smalley, Collections and Research Manager, Saco Museum, Saco, Maine, via Bremerton, Washington

Growing up in Bremerton, Washington, I usually attended the Rodeo Drive-In theater in Port Orchard, Washington—about twenty-five minutes from my house. I never really went until I was a teenager, and then it was usually with my friends. We loved seeing films at the drive-in because we could be as loud as we wished inside the car. At indoor theaters, we were usually shushed or given very unpleasant looks (admittedly, not undeserved) from other movie patrons due to our loud, raucous laughter and usually distracting commentary. I remember going to the Rodeo and seeing Will Ferrell's *Old School* and getting into a popcorn fight. We spent at least an hour vacuuming out my 1990 Chevy Beretta GT the next day.

The drive-in, just like in the 1950s and 1960s, was a place where teenagers could be themselves without bothering anyone. We could be just as obnoxious as we liked, or quiet or anything. I think this freedom, as well as access to a car, is one of those milestones that every teenager experiences. Now, a decade later as a Saco resident, the Saco Drive-In theater has a special place for me, not just as a movie theater but also as a tangible piece of Saco history and cultural capital. Very few businesses survive five years in the twenty-first-century world of today; however, the Saco Drive-In has managed to exist for seventy-four years, entertaining thousands of people. That is not something many businesses can even dream of bragging about. This place matters.

When my friend Ry Russell asked me to join him and our friend Justin Chenette to work on fundraising for the drive-in, I said yes but didn't really know what I was agreeing to. I knew I wanted to save a historic landmark but was not sure how to go about it. Justin, Ry and I planned a large yard sale at the drive-in that brought in about $1,400. It was a lot of work, and we were really proud of the money we made! Next, Ry set up a comedy fundraiser at the Gold Room in Portland, again raising another couple thousand. We were still about $70,000 short of buying a digital projector. When Honda approached us with "Project Drive-In," I was floored. I couldn't believe that someone was stepping in, someone like Honda, a huge automaker, with what seemed like a golden ticket. The answer to all our problems. Of course, I knew this was not going to be a quick way to make money or get a digital projector by any means—but this had an endgame: a digital projector.

Justin and I spent many long evenings at the drive-in with Ry working with Honda to film promotional pieces for the whole project. It was summer, and hot and sticky—black flies and mosquitoes were everywhere—but it was worth it. I could feel it. I wrote our informational paragraph for the website and gave Ry the phrase "A vote for the Saco Drive-In is as American as apple pie!" The promotion began, and we took off like a shot, with no concept of pacing ourselves. We were going for the gold, and we were going full force. I began working on an e-book fundraiser as a way to celebrate the history of the Saco Drive-In, as well as capturing the experiences of people who have attended the theater over the past seventy-four years. It was hard work, promoting the theater every day on Facebook. The Saco Drive-In was on the tip of my tongue and the first thought in my brain all of the 2013 summer. That thirty-day period in August was the hardest I have ever worked for something. I helped Ry with sending out press releases for our events and for the drive-in. I wanted every single newspaper in the Southern Maine area, and farther if I could get it, to hear our name and want us to win. I wanted to inspire people. I wanted them to see the value of this great theater started by an Italian immigrant, by someone who came to the United States and sought to build his own American dream—and did it. This drive-in theater is not just a fenced piece of land with a screen—it's the definition of what we strive for in our lives, to build up ourselves, to make our own way. It was a dream for Eugene Boragine, and it's a dream for Ry Russell (as well as Justin and me). I probably talked about the drive-in until I was blue in the face.

I was completely shocked by how many people came forward and wanted to help us, wanted to get the word out, wrote about us and more. The Maine Historical Society wrote a blog about the Saco Drive-In and the "Project Drive-In" competition. It felt like everyone wanted us to win and that we were the best. As September 9 neared, I got really nervous. I began to convince myself that if we didn't win, it was OK, we gave it our best—and that's what really counts. I reminded myself I gave it my best effort and I should not get too upset when we did not win; after all, other drive-ins are in gigantic metropolitan areas with three times our voting population. I remember on September 12 when Ry called me while I was at work at the Saco Museum. I answered my phone, and he said, "So, we did it."

I did not understand what he meant.

"We did what?"

"We won."

"We did not. You're just building me up to let me down gently."

"Camille, Camille. We won. We won the digital projector."

Courtesy of Jon Emack.

I could hear the tears of joy in his voice as I started to cry and kept asking, "Are you sure? Are you sure?" Soon, we were both crying and hardly able to understand each other. He was finally able to tell me that we were having a party at the drive-in that evening, and I said I would be there. I then called Justin, who hadn't heard from Ry yet, and the tears started all over again as he said he would pick me up for the victory party later. Poor Ry became so bombarded with phone calls and texts that he had to turn his phone off for the rest of the evening. It was surreal.

Justin and I arrived at the drive-in about 4:30 that afternoon and joined in the toast with the staff and other drive-in supporters. The gates opened early that evening to start letting people in who wanted to celebrate and watch a free showing of *Grown Ups 2*. All of the newspapers were present, several news crews, Honda—it really did not seem true. It was one of the last ninety-five-degree days of the summer and no better time to be standing at the drive-in, celebrating a victory. Six months before, in April, I remembered sitting around a conference table with Ry and Justin saying, "We'll do this. We have to. I mean, we can do this. Right?" All of the anxiety, tears and stress felt so worth it that September evening. We were the top drive-in in America, and we won. More so, the Saco Drive-In could continue into its seventy-fifth season. All I could think of was, "What would Eugene think of this now? How proud would he be that the community of families and children he loved so much and welcomed with open arms to his theater rallied behind the drive-in?" I could only imagine that he was smiling with Helen that evening and that we had done well.

CONCLUSION

From their inception in 1932 until today, drive-in theaters are still known as places for people to enjoy time together. While drive-in theaters are few and far between these days, their patrons are passionate and enjoy the vision Richard Hollingshead Jr. created. The Saco Drive-In opened as Maine's first drive-in (then the Motor-In Theater) on July 15, 1939, and offered outdoor cinema from the comfort and privacy of one's own vehicle. While drive-in theaters opened from coast to coast and the ozoner experienced its peak of popularity in the mid-twentieth century, people today in the twenty-first century still motor into the remaining so-called passion pits to enjoy outdoor films with their families. The magic of the outdoor film truly cast a spell over moviegoers, both for patrons of the Saco Drive-In and at other ozoners nationwide. Despite the differences in time, technology and schedules, people are still looking for affordable ways to spend time with one another.

Since the post–World War II era, and the societal push for family togetherness, more emphasis has been put on the family as a unit. In order to stay properly connected, that unit has to work together and spend time together. Despite the recession in the 1970s and hardships in the 1980s, the drive-in has been reborn from the ashes and reestablished itself as a family environment that offers entertainment at an affordable price for all. Located on the busy roadway known as Route 1 or the Portland Road, the Saco Drive-In also fell victim to changing times and had to reinvent itself as a family-friendly, top-quality theater. It's quite remarkable that the drive-in has truly stood the test of time, enduring the cyclical nature of economic

Saco Drive-In logo.

boom and bust over the twentieth and twenty-first centuries. Much like their 1950s counterparts, families today do not always want to get dressed up or feel pressured to look a certain way to go out together. The drive-in offers a safe, private space for families to be together and simply enjoy one another's company without judgment. Whether it is 1939, 1959 or 2009, the passion for film and family time continues.

GLOSSARY

amusement: The state of being amused or entertained by something. In the nineteenth century, amusements included fairs, walks in the park, events on the pier in Old Orchard Beach and many other things. In the twentieth and twenty-first centuries, amusements include films, plays, games and other content.

"Auto Mile": In Saco, the "auto mile" refers to a stretch of Route 1, or the Portland Road, with a high concentration of car dealerships.

Biddeford, Maine: Founded in 1631, along with Saco, Biddeford developed into a burgeoning mill city by the mid-nineteenth century. Textiles made at the Pepperrell and Laconia Manufacturing Companies traveled around the world, known by the trademark dragon logo or "chop." By the 1880s, many French Canadian immigrants had moved to the area and pursued factory work. By the time the Saco Drive-In opened in 1939, downtown Biddeford was a bustling town with many shops and businesses. The textile industry moved out of Biddeford in the early 2000s, and since then, the town has been renovating its large textile factory buildings into multi-use buildings.

Biddeford Pool, Maine: Biddeford Pool was one of the early settled areas of Biddeford in the seventeenth century. Just as Saco's Ferry Beach became a place of refuge and seaside cottages, so did Biddeford Pool. Currently, there are a variety of homes along with public beaches.

Captain Richard Bonython: In 1630, Captain Richard Bonython received a royal patent to settle the Camp Ellis/Saco side of land at the confluence of the Saco River and Atlantic Ocean, across from Captain Richard Vines's patented land. The same rules applied: Bonython had seven years to have fifty people settle in the area.

Eugene Boragine: Born in Naples, Italy, at age ten, he immigrated with his family to New York, New York.

Bridgton, Maine: A town located fifty miles northwest of Saco, Bridgton is the home of one of the state's five still-operating drive-in theaters.

Cascades Restaurant: Also known as Cascades Inn and Cabins, this resort of sorts was built in 1929 in what was then a hayfield on Route 1. Cascades offered small cabins, advertised as the utmost quality and unparalleled luxury. Behind where the restaurant and cabins stood is Cascade Falls, a tumbling brook where visitors took strolls while vacationing at the inn. Still visible today, an empty bear cage sits where a live bear used to entertain visitors. The building was demolished in 2010; however, the trails for Cascade Falls are still maintained by Saco Bay Trails and open for hiking.

Cinemagic Theaters: This cinema chain operates ninety-one screens in eight locations across Maine, New Hampshire and Massachusetts. Cinemagic offers digital projection, as well as digital sound and the newest technology. Just as drive-ins offered sporting events and other events on their big screens, the majority of twenty-first-century indoor theaters do as well.

concession stand: This permanent or, in some cases, semipermanent structure sells food items during events such as movies, sporting events and other entertainments. At the Saco Drive-In, the concession stand is a permanent structure located in the center of the theater. Attached to the concession building is the projection room, as well as men's and women's bathrooms. At the Saco Drive-In, this building is original, with very few alterations made to the building aside from painting the inside. In the 1950s, a mural painted by Eugene Boragine adorned the walls; today, it's simply white. The stand offers hamburgers, hot dogs, chicken fingers, French fries, pizza and sometimes specialty items like fried dough.

GLOSSARY

drive-in: Invented by Richard Hollingshead Jr. in 1932, a drive-in theater is a place to watch films outdoors in the comfort of your own car. Parking stalls are situated with compact cars in the front of the theater and larger cars in the back as a way for all to view the films comfortably. In 1939, when the Saco Drive-In on Route 1 opened, film fans heard the film through one large central speaker. In the twenty-first century, one simply tunes his or her radio to a certain station and can control the volume. Many people bring their own radios and do not even use their car radios.

dummy rail: The Old Orchard and Ferry Beach Railroad Company built a "dummy" rail line that ran from the Boston and Maine Railroad depot across the beach. Visitors connected to steamers going upriver or to ferries heading to Biddeford Pool from this line. The small steam engine was referred to as a "dummy" due to its size and small engine.

Ferry Beach Park Association: In 1901, Dr. Quillen Hamilton Shinn located the wooded pine grove on Ferry Beach for the Universalists' annual retreat. The property was purchased from the Boston and Maine Railroad, and in 1909, the Ferry Beach Park Association was established.

Flag Pond Road: Saco's Flag Pond Road is a stretch of road that is located a half mile from the Saco Drive-In off Route 1. This neighborhood is in the more rural section of Saco and was home to many farms and dairies.

Sir Fernando Gorges: The second colonial governor of Maine, Gorges founded the Province of Maine in 1622. He funded the failed Popham Colony on the Kennebec River, near Augusta. Gorges funded many voyages to the state, as well as settlements. The fort located on Hog Island Ledge in Casco Bay is named "Gorges" after him.

hardtop: By the 1950s, indoor theaters were referred to as hardtops.

Richard Hollingshead Jr.: Hollingshead invented the drive-in theater by placing a 1928 Kodak film projector on the hood of his car. He tested the projection at various angles and in varying weather conditions, ultimately creating a theater of cars in a staggered pattern parked in front of a large outdoor screen. Hollingshead applied for and received a patent for the drive-in on May 16, 1933.

indoor theater: To distinguish drive-in theaters from more traditional movie theaters, the latter is referred to as an indoor theater. Originally, indoor theaters were typically owned by one of the big five Hollywood studios and only showed that company's films: Paramount, 20th Century Fox, MGM, RKO and Warner Brothers.

Kennebunk Drive-In: The Kennebunk Drive-In opened in the 1950s and closed in 1980. The theater's maximum capacity was four hundred.

Kennebunk, Maine: Kennebunk is a coastal town in southern Maine, located ten miles south of Saco. Here, the Kennebunk Drive-In was located until it closed in 1980.

Madawaska, Maine: Located in Washington County, Madawaska is located 361 miles north of Saco.

newsreel: Before the nightly news occurred on televisions across America, newsreels played before films at both indoor theaters and drive-ins. Newsreels contained a summary of global events and often included various propaganda as necessary (during World War II, for example) and advertisements. As the name describes, the news was in a film cell format and played like a film reel on the projector.

Ocean Park: Founded in 1881, Ocean Park developed a summer resort originally for the Free Will Baptists. The Ocean Park Association, much like Ferry Beach, offered lectures and quiet camping in cabins, as well as worship in a temple. Ocean Park celebrates its 134th anniversary in 2014.

Old Orchard Beach: Old Orchard Beach was first settled by Thomas Rogers in 1657, and the town is named for an apple orchard that grew on the high ground above the sand. Old Orchard was part of Saco for many years, until Saco's neglect of the area led citizens to push for their own independent town in the 1880s. The first Old Orchard Beach town hall was built in 1900. The town enjoys a bustling tourist economy with beautiful beach views.

ozoner: This term is slang for a drive-in theater and refers to the outdoor experience of the drive-in.

panoramic screen: This screen gave a large, unbroken view of films at the drive-in. The drive-in screens are much larger than the traditional sixteen- by nineteen-foot screen of an indoor theater.

passion pit: Another slang term for a drive-in theater, this one refers to the romance and sometimes physical intimacy that occurred between teenagers in the privacy of the car during a drive-in movie.

Portland Road: Also known as Route 1, Elm Street and many other names. Route 1 travels through Saco on Elm Street, which turns into Main Street, which becomes Portland Road. It is appropriately named, as it is the way to Portland, Maine.

Portland Twin Drive-In: Located in Scarborough, Maine, and on Route 1, the Portland Twin Drive-In opened in 1949 with one screen. In 1968, a second screen was added and the size was increased. By 1980, the maximum capacity was seven hundred. However, like many drive-ins, the Portland Twin closed in 1986 and was torn down by 1990.

Pride's Corner Drive-In: Located in Westbrook, Maine, this drive-in theater opened in 1953. This theater is currently operational and shows first-run films all summer long.

Bud and Lilla Priest: Parents of contributor David Priest, Bud and Lilla worked with Helen and Eugene Boragine at the Saco Drive-In in the 1950s. Thanks to them, we have snapshots of those early years of the Saco Drive-In.

Project Drive-In: Honda's campaign during the summer of 2013 to donate five digital projectors to five drive-in theaters. Popular vote determined the winners. Honda ultimately gave away nine digital projectors instead of five. The winners are listed here alphabetically:

Cherry Bowl Drive-In, Honor, Michigan
Graham Drive-In, Graham, Texas
McHenry Outdoor Theater, McHenry, Illinois
Monetta Drive-In, Monetta, South Carolina
99 Drive-In, Newberg, Oregon
Ocala Drive-In, Ocala, Florida
Saco Drive-In, Saco, Maine

Starlite Drive-In, Cadet, Missouri
Stateline Drive-In, Elizabethton, Tennessee

Honda is still accepting donations via its "Project Drive-In" website in an effort to raise money for the other 140 drive-in theaters that participated in the contest. http://projectdrivein.com.

projector: The projector is the equipment used to project the film onto the panoramic screen. From the 1950s through the 1990s, the projector took up nearly the entire projection booth. A projectionist set up the film before the movie was set to start and kept an eye on the machine while it was running. If a bug got stuck to the film or the cells broke, the projectionist would fix the film so the show could continue. In the twenty-first century, no film is required, and films are obtained digitally.

RCA: Radio Corporation of America was founded in 1919, with David Sarnoff as the first general manager of the company. In 1986, the trademark was purchased by Sony Music and Technicolor. Hollingshead worked with RCA on various speaker patterns for his first drive-in.

Route 1: A nearly three-hundred-year-old roadway between Saco and Portland developed as the main roadway between Maine and Florida before the construction of I-95. Much like Route 66, Route 1 was designed to carry traffic north and south, with various businesses and places to stay along the way; however, Route 1 does not share the fame that Route 66 does. Route 66 is a well-known American roadway, referred to as the "Main Street of America." It was developed in November 1926 and is 2,448 miles long. Route 1 starts in Miami, Florida, and terminates in Fort Kent, Maine (or in the reverse order if you are traveling south). Route 1 as a whole is 2,369 miles long.

Saco, Maine: Founded in 1630 along with Biddeford, Saco grew to be a burgeoning mill town with the York Manufacturing Company in full swing on Factory Island by 1840. In 1811, the local secondary school became Thornton Academy after a generous donation from Thomas G. Thornton. It is still a renowned high school today. The York Manufacturing Company closed in the 1950s, and Saco endured a small economic repression. Still, shops along Main Street continued to grow as people found homes in the area. Saco has longtime philanthropic and historical groups such as

Sweetser (1828), the Saco Museum (formerly York Institute, 1866), the Wardwell Home (1878) and the Dyer Library (1881).

Scarborough, Maine: On the historic Route 1, Scarborough is a short eight miles north of Saco. Here, the Portland Twin Drive-In was located. Scarborough was founded in 1635, only four years after Saco.

Skowhegan Drive-In: Located in Skowhegan, Maine, this drive-in opened in 1954. This theater is currently operational.

Skowhegan, Maine: This town is located 109 miles north of the city of Saco.

Starlight Drive-In: This drive-in located in Madawaska, Maine, opened twenty years after the drive-in boom in 1973. This drive-in is still operational and entertains families from all over northern Maine.

talkies: The earliest films in American history were short, silent films with just music as an accompaniment. When sound was added, they were called "talkies."

ticket booth: Tickets were sold, as well as hot dogs, at the ticket booth at the Saco Drive-In. A patron simply pulled up to the booth and paid his or her admission and then was directed by an usher to a parking stall in the theater.

Helen Toth: Wife of Saco Drive-In owner Eugene Boragine, Helen was born on March 7, 1902, in New York City. The pair met and was married in New York. The couple lived in Saco from at least 1947 through 1961, until Eugene's death. After the death of her husband, Helen moved to North Palm Beach, Florida, and lived there until her death on August 26, 1998, at age ninety-six.

usher: A drive-in usher assisted in directing cars to parking locations within the theater. After RCA personal speakers became available, ushers installed and uninstalled the speakers from cars—preferably before the patron forgot the speakers were still attached!

Captain Richard Vines: Captain Richard Vines, sponsored by Sir Fernando Gorges, traveled to the mouth of the Saco River in 1615 to investigate the area. He was ordered to winter at the location and see if the area would make a suitable fishing village. As his winter was successful, Vines traveled back and forth between England and the Camp Ellis/Biddeford Pool area. He received a royal patent for settlement in 1630.

Westbrook: A suburb of Maine's largest city, Portland, Westbrook is located seventeen miles from the city of Saco.

zoning ordinance: These written regulations and laws define how a geographic area within a city, town or county can be used. Areas can be zoned, for example, for commercial or residential use and can be rezoned at the discretion of the planning board for the city, county or state.

Appendix

DRIVE-INS IN MAINE

Maine boasted at least forty-seven drive-in theaters between 1939 and 1955. A few of the theaters—at least eight—opened in 1949, while the majority of others were open by 1955. Just as the boom started in 1949, the rapid cessation of theaters occurred in the 1980s. However, five Maine drive-ins remain open today, and two have converted to digital film projection at this time.

**indicates the drive-in is currently operational as of 2014*

Acton Drive-In, U.S. Route 109 and Twelfth Street, Acton, Maine

Opened: 1949
The Acton Drive-In was open for only a few seasons. The theater was torn down, and the Acton Fairgrounds now stand in its place.

Auburn Drive-In, 254 Old Portland Road, Auburn, Maine

Opened: 1949
Closed: 1988
The Auburn Drive-In originally opened in 1949 under the name the Danville Drive-In. Like many theaters, the theater changed names in 1950 during the ozoner boom. The Auburn Drive-In held three hundred cars. Currently, two mobile homes exist on the property.

St. Croix Valley Drive-In, U.S. Route 1, Baring, Maine

Opened: 1954
Closed: 1995
The St. Croix Valley Drive-In was located in Baring, Maine, about 236 miles from Saco, on the border of Maine and Canada, with a car capacity of three hundred. As drive-ins are large, clear properties, a warehouse currently sits at this site on U.S. Route 1.

Belfast Drive-In, Route 3, Belfast, Maine

Not much is known about the Belfast Drive-In aside from the fact that it probably held four hundred cars at maximum capacity. There are currently a shopping plaza and an auto dealership at the corner of the former entrance road off Route 3.

Brewer Drive-In, Brewer, Maine

Opened: July 4, 1950
Closed: 1986
Not much is known about the Brewer Drive-In aside from its opening and closing dates. The theater supposedly held seven hundred cars and was demolished in May 1987.

Bridgton Twin Drive-In, 383 Portland Road (Route 302), Bridgton, Maine

Opened: 1957
The Bridgton Twin Drive-In is still open and has a digital projector. In 2000, the drive-in added a second screen so two films can be shown at once. The theater can hold 495 cars and is a local attraction. Its admission is $7.50 for ages twelve and up and $5.00 for ages five through eleven with a special $15.00 per carload on Fridays, Saturdays and holidays. For more information about its films, check out its Facebook page.

Brunswick Drive-In, Brunswick, Maine

Opened: 1950
Closed: 1984
Not much is known about this drive-in theater aside from the location and opening/closing dates. The Brunswick Drive-In opened during the height of

drive-in popularity and closed about the same time the majority of ozoners closed their gates forever.

Dorseyland Drive-In, Highway 89, Caribou, Maine

Opened: 1962
Closed: 1989
At some point, the Dorseyland Drive-In changed its name to the Hilltop Drive-In, possibly in its later years as an attempt to revitalize the theater. Surprisingly, this theater opened much later than most drive-ins and lasted only twenty-seven years.

Polaris Drive-In, Maine Street, Caribou, Maine

Opened: 1949
Closed: 1982
The Polaris Drive-In opened during the early boom of drive-ins and was sold to Charlie Brooks in 1966 and, later, Larry Cyr in 1981, according to the drive-in database (drive-in.com). This ozoner could hold 470 cars and is now an open field.

Cornish Drive-In, 233 Main Street (Route 25), Cornish, Maine

Closed: 1980s
Not much is known about this drive-in aside from speculation that it closed in the 1980s. Currently, there is a self-storage facility on the property, aptly titled "Cornish Drive In Storage."

Midway Drive-In, U.S. Route 100, Detroit, Maine

Not much is known about this theater, either, aside from the fact that the theater possibly had a capacity of three hundred cars. Detroit is a small town in Maine outside Pittsfield. As of 2004, the land was for sale.

Bowdoin Drive-In, East Brunswick, Maine

Supposedly, this drive-in held four hundred cars at maximum capacity and was located at Cook's Corner.

Drive-In, U.S. Route 1, Ellsworth Falls, Maine

There isn't anything really known about this drive-in. Its capacity is listed at twenty cars, so perhaps it was just a small field turned into a drive-in for a short period of time.

Estcourt Drive-In, 1355 Rue de la Frontière, Estcourt Station, Maine

Interestingly, this drive-in is located in Estcourt Station, which is a town in the International Boundary of Maine and Quebec. The town has no regular access road into Maine without crossing the border into Quebec and then proceeding into Maine. There is not much information available about this drive-in aside from the fact that it existed in this area.

Boundary Line Drive-In, 54 Boundary Line Road, Fort Fairfield, Maine

Opened: Prior to 1955
Not much else is known about this drive-in aside from its location and possible three-hundred-car capacity.

Fort Kent Drive-In, Highway 161, Fort Kent, Maine

Not much is known about the Fort Kent Drive-In aside from the fact that it had a four-hundred-car capacity. The theater was located off Highway 161 on Drive-In Road.

Bangor Twin Drive-In, Hammond Street (Route 2), Hermon, Maine

Closed: 1987
The Bangor Twin Drive-In had two screens and two concession stands, although one of the concession stands has been torn down. This ozoner had the typical three-hundred-car maximum capacity.

Borderland Drive-In, U.S. Route 1, Houlton, Maine

Opened: 1949
Closed: 1985
This drive-in opened in 1949, as did many drive-ins in Maine and on U.S. Route 1. The ozoner had a four-hundred-car capacity.

Kennebunk Drive-In, 62 Portland Road (U.S. Route 1), Kennebunk, Maine

Opened: 1950
Closed: 1980
Another drive-in on U.S. Route 1, the Kennebunk Drive-In had a four-hundred-car capacity. Currently, there is a series of medical and other health-related offices where the ozoner used to sit.

Kittery York Drive-In, U.S. Route 1, Kittery, Maine

There are no details available about this drive-in aside from the fact that it was located on U.S. Route 1. Since the drive-in was demolished, the property has become an outlet mall.

Lewiston Drive-In, Sabbatus Road, 1 Lewiston, Maine

Opened: 1949
Closed: 1985
This one-screen outdoor theater had a maximum car capacity of five hundred, one of the larger drive-ins in the state of Maine. Currently, the property is a mobile home park.

Lisbon Drive-In, Lisbon Street and Foss Road, Lewiston, Maine

There are no documented dates about the Lisbon Drive-In, but it is speculated that the ozoner could hold eight hundred cars. Now, the property is the home of a beverage distribution warehouse.

Greenland Drive-In, Machias, Maine

There are no documented dates for this drive-in; however, it was also attached to a motel. Here, guests could stay at the motel and see movies at the drive-in.

Madawaska Drive-In, Madawaska, Maine

Nothing is listed about this drive-in, aside from the fact that it was located in Madawaska. Perhaps this drive-in shut down just prior to the Skylite Drive-In opening.

Skylite Drive-In and Fox Theater, 304 Eleventh Avenue, Madawaska, Maine*

Opened: 1973
This drive-in was still open as of 2013 and had not announced the opening date for the 2014 season at the time of printing. The theater does have a Facebook page that is regularly posted to. Also, the theater is linked to the indoor Fox Theater, which shows movies in the drive-in's off season.

Augusta Drive-In, Route 202, Manchester, Maine

There is no information available about this drive-in, aside from speculation that it had a nine-hundred-car capacity. This drive-in was located just outside Maine's capital city of Augusta.

Katahdin Drive-In, Highway 157, Mattawankeag, Maine

There is no information available about this drive-in, either, as far as dates go; however it was located close to Mount Katahdin, Maine's highest point. This drive-in probably drew locals from the surrounding towns, as well as tourists who camped in Baxter State Park.

Milo Drive-In, Elm Street, Milo, Maine

This ozoner also does not have any information available beyond its location on Elm Street and possible three-hundred-car maximum capacity. Milo is located 258 miles north and slightly west of Saco.

Naples Drive-In, Route 3, Naples, Maine

There is no available information about this drive-in aside from the fact that it possibly opened in 1949 and closed shortly thereafter. According to the database on drive-in.com, the drive-in was located where Sydney's Restaurant and Pub is today.

Windham Drive-In, Highway 102 and Drive-In Lane, North Windham, Maine

Opened: 1949
Closed: 1984
The Windham Drive-In had one screen and a maximum capacity of three hundred cars. This ozoner appeared to follow the same timeline as most outdoor theaters by opening in the mid-twentieth century and closing in the 1980s. It's noted that the property was for sale in 2001; it is a car dealership.

Norway Drive-In, Highway 26, Norway, Maine

This drive-in does not have any readily available information aside from possibly having a three-hundred-car maximum capacity. It most likely opened in the late 1940s or early 1950s.

Presque Isle Drive-In, Presque Isle, Maine

The Presque Isle Drive-In probably opened in the late 1940s or early 1950s. Not much is known aside from the fact that it possibly had a 350-car maximum capacity.

Rockland Drive-In, Rockport, Maine

This drive-in most likely opened in 1949 or 1950, as it's noted the theater survived some damage due to Hurricane Edna in 1954. This ozoner has been defunct since 1985 and was demolished.

Rumford Drive-In, 56 Franklin Street, Rumford, Maine

Opened: 1949
Closed: 1985

The Rumford Drive-In had a five-hundred-car maximum capacity and opened at the same time as other drive-ins in the state of Maine. After the theater was closed in 1985, the buildings and screen were demolished in 1986.

Saco Drive-In, 969 Portland Road, Saco, Maine*

Opened: 1939
The Saco Drive-In is still operating on U.S. Route 1 through Saco. The theater features a concession stand and a digital projector plus a five-hundred-car maximum capacity. For more information, visit its Facebook page or website: www.thesacodrivein.com.

Sanford Drive-In, Main Street and Breary Avenue, Sanford, Maine

Opened: 1954
Closed: 1975
The Sanford Drive-In had a three-hundred-car maximum capacity and one screen. In 1953, the ozoner was sold to E.M. Loews, and it was completely defunct by 1975. The outdoor theater was demolished, and the property is now home to the Breary Apartments.

Portland Twin Drive-In, U.S. Route 1, Scarborough, Maine

Opened: 1949
Closed: 1986
In 1968, the Portland Twin Drive-In added a second screen and increased to a seven-hundred-car maximum capacity. Located on U.S. Route 1 like many of Maine's other drive-ins, the Portland Twin drew residents from Scarborough and Portland and probably those from Saco who desired to see different films than were available at the Saco Drive-In. The theater was defunct in 1986 and razed in 2003. Now, the property is host to a car wash and restaurants.

Skowhegan Drive-In, 201 Waterville Road, Skowhegan, Maine*

Opened: 1954
The Skowhegan Drive-In is still an open and active drive-in theater. This ozoner does not currently have a digital projector; however, on its website,

it does have a link for donations: www.skowhegandrivein.com. The theater charges seven dollars for ages twelve and up and four dollars for ages eleven and younger. The Skowhegan Drive-In has a three-hundred-car maximum capacity and entertains many families all year long.

Ellsworth-Trenton Drive-In, Bar Harbor Road, Trenton, Maine

Opened: 1949
Closed: 1950
Reopened: 1952
Closed: 1984
The Ellsworth-Trenton Drive-In originally opened in 1949 as the Auto View Drive-In, similar to Saco's original title of Motor-In Theater. In 1952, the ozoner reopened with the name Ellsworth-Trenton Drive-In and remained in operation until its official closing in 1984. The site is now host to a market.

Van Buren Drive-In, Highway 165, Van Buren, Maine

Not much is known about this ozoner located in the small town of Van Buren aside from the fact that it possibly had a five-hundred-car maximum capacity.

Prides Corner Drive-In, 651 Bridgton Road, Westbrook, Maine*

Open: 1953
The Prides Corner Drive-In has a maximum car capacity of 550 and is still an open drive-in today. However, this drive-in has not converted to digital and has started fundraising at this time. (See its Facebook page for details or to donate.) The Tenevian brothers bought the parcel of land in Westbrook in 1952, when they returned home from World War II, and the theater opened in May 1953. The ozoner still entertains thousands of families today.

Enfield Drive-In, West Enfield, Maine

Opened: 1949
Closed: 1985
This small ozoner had a maximum capacity of two hundred cars. The theater was demolished sometime after 1985, and the property is currently a mobile home park.

Jay Hill Drive-In, Highway 4, Wilton, Maine

There is no readily available information for this ozoner. The theater probably opened in the late 1940s or early 1950s and closed in the 1980s.

Winslow Drive-In, 447 Augusta Road, Winslow, Maine

Opened: 1949
Closed: 1986
This ozoner originally opened in 1949 as the Waterville Drive-In. It closed in 1949 and reopened as the Winslow Drive-In within the year, but by 1986, the theater was defunct. This theater boasted a 550-car maximum capacity. The property is now a mobile home park.

Pines Drive-In, Woolwich, Maine

Opened: 1947
Closed: 1950
Not much is known about this ozoner; perhaps it did not have a successful market in Woolwich.

Yarmouth Drive-In, U.S. Route 1, Yarmouth, Maine

Not much is known about this drive-in, and the site is now a supermarket.

Sources:

Drive-On-In, Inc. "Drive-In Theater Database." Last modified January 2014. www.driveins.com (accessed March 26, 2014).

Martin, Adam. "Cinema Tour: Cinema History Around the World." Vision Entertainment. Last modified January 2014. http://www.cinematour.com (accessed March 26, 2014).

NOTES

Feature 1

The Saco Drive-In Opens

1. This is the first advertisement for the Saco Drive-In, then the Motor-In Theatre, published in a newspaper. It advertises the opening evening with multiple shows. Motor-In Theatre Advertisement, *Biddeford Daily Journal,* July 15, 1939, McArthur Library Archives, Biddeford, Maine.
2. According to Wright, Route 1 was referred to by residents as the "King's Highway." Many colonists did not use this roadway because they did not appreciate being ordered to spend money to build it, so large sections of road were finished just enough to pass as a road. In 1911, Route 1 was renamed the "Quebec-Miami International Highway." Wright, *Route 1,* 3.
3. Segrave, *Drive-In Theaters*, 2–3.
4. Ibid., 72.
5. Cohen, "Forgotten Audiences," 470–86.
6. Segrave, *Drive-In Theaters*, 20–23.

A Brief History of Saco

7. Captain Martin Pring, an English navigator, explored the Saco Bay region under the direction of geographer Richard Hakluyt in 1606. Pring wrote that the river was named "Shawakotoc" and had "trees growing on each side soe crosse with their boughs and bodies" such that no vessel could travel on the river. The name "Shawakotoc" is one Pring most likely

learned from the Abenaki on the riverbanks. Fairfield, *Sands, Spindles, and Steeples*, 5.

8. Ibid., 3.
9. Ibid., 6.
10. Ibid., 7. In 1631, the entire settlement was known as Saco, and settlers immediately built the first meetinghouse on the western bank of the river (near where the University of New England now stands). This meetinghouse served as both a house of worship and a political space for settlement-related decisions. Residents on the east bank traveled across the Saco River a minimum of once per week for worship and town meetings. At this time, many people referred to living in "East Saco" or "West Saco."
11 Ibid., 10.
12. Ibid., 12. In the mid-eighteenth century, Colonel Thomas Cutts, former clerk of Sir William Pepperrel, purchased Indian Island for $2,000. He saw the economic potential in the land, located just under the falls of the Saco River. Here, Native Americans usually fished and traded; however, after Cutts purchased the land, their rights were seen as customary only. Cutts then cleared the land of trees and brush to make room for his future business ventures. Utilizing the Lottery Bridges, as well as his wharf rights and shipbuilding, Cutts became the wealthiest man in the community and the father of Saco's industrial heritage.
13. Ibid., 13. At a town meeting that year (1718), citizens decided to pay an additional forty dollars to support a minister and to change the name of the settlement from Saco to Biddeford, regardless of on which side of the river one lived.
14. Ibid., 30.
15. Ibid. The citizens also constructed Old Orchard Road, located off Ferry Road. This roadway is about a mile or so long, connecting Saco and Old Orchard Beach. In 1657, a good twenty years after Saco was founded, Thomas Rogers called the area the "Garden by the Sea." In 1660, Rogers planted the apple orchard for which the town is named. Old Orchard Beach officially incorporated as a town in 1883.
16. Ibid., 40. The eastern settlement then became Pepperrellborough, named for the generous bequests of land made by Sir William Pepperrell. In 1805, Pepperrellborough returned to the original shortened name of Saco.
17. Ibid., 48.

Taking a Walk on the Boardwalk

18. Mitman, "Hay Fever Holiday," 603.
19. Bassett, "Documenting Recreation," 563.

20. Fairfield, " Old Orchard," 228.
21. Ibid., 229.
22. Ibid., 230.
23. Gross, "Cars, Postcards, and Patriotism," 80.
24. Records of the Ferry Beach Association from 1901 through 1959 include scrapbooks, legal documents and financial records, chronicling the goings-on of the association for a half century. The Ferry Beach Park Association is still a very active group that primarily serves the residents of Ferry Beach. Bassett, "Documenting Recreation," 560.
25. Fairfield, "Old Orchard," 240.

Driving to the Drive-In

26. With the introduction of the automobile, headlines in newspapers often depicted accidents and notes about maximum speeds on local roads. Fairfield describes the automobile as a reason why people often owned smaller homes—due to the expense of owning an automobile. Fairfield, *Sands, Spindles, and Steeples*, 380.
27. Ibid.
28. Wright, *Route 1*, 5.
29. Ibid., 7.
30. Ibid., 9.
31. Richard Hollingshead Jr. lived at 212 Thomas Avenue in Camden, New Jersey. He custom-built a thirty- by sixty-foot screen for the projector on top of his car. Segrave, *Drive-In Theaters*, 24–25.
32. Everett and McKeon, *Cinema Under the Stars*, 26.
33. Hollingshead received the patent for his "Drive-In Theater" on May 16, 1933: Patent Number 1,909,537. This patent was guaranteed for seventeen years and meant Hollingshead could collect royalties from anyone seeking to build a drive-in theater. However, after drive-in theaters became national, the Supreme Court ruled that the drive-in was really not patentable since cars could be set up only in a certain pattern and Hollingshead's drive-in was not unique. Segrave, *Drive-In Theaters*, 27.
34. Everett and McKeon, *Cinema Under the Stars*, 28.
35. The baby boom between 1946 and 1964 reversed the steadily declining birthrates of previous decades. According to Lynne Spigel, this "revitalized the nuclear family as a basic social construct." Between 1929 and 1941, the declining birthrate slowed the development of residential housing. With the Great Depression followed shortly by World War II, housing was unable to expand until after the war. Spigel, *Make Room for TV*, 33.
36. Ibid., 50.

37. Ibid., 34.
38. Ibid., 32.
39. Ibid., 101.

Enjoying a Double Feature at the Saco Drive-In

40. Boragine's wife, Helen Toth, was born on March 7, 1902. United States Federal Census 1930, roll 1548, page 44B, Queens, New York, Household of Eugene V. Boragine at age thirty-one, accessed online at Ancestry.com, July 14, 2013.
41. According to Boragine's obituary, he died at his home on the Portland Road on Monday, November 28, 1961. He was born on December 27, 1898, to Guy and Filomena Varone Boragine. Boragine served as noble grand for the International Order of the Odd Fellows in New York City, as well as belonged to the Orchard Lodge of Free and Accepted Masons and the Kora Shrine Temple in Lewiston, Maine. At his death, he had two sisters living in Rhode Island and a brother living in Swanee, Massachusetts. Eugene V. Boragine Obituary, *Biddeford-Saco Journal*, November 30, 1961, McArthur Library Archives, Biddeford, Maine.
42. Segrave, *Drive-In Theaters*, 28.
43. *Biddeford-Saco Business Directory*, 1954, Roy P. Fairfield Maine History Room, Dyer Library, Saco, Maine.
44. Everett and McKeon, *Cinema Under the Stars*, 65.
45. Segrave, *Drive-In Theaters*, 40.
46. Everett and McKeon, *Cinema Under the Stars*, 25.
47. Ibid., 11.
48. Segrave, *Drive-In Theaters*, 40.
49. Everett and McKeon, *Cinema Under the Stars*, 49.
50. Motor-In Theater Advertisement, *Biddeford Daily Journal*, May 1940, McArthur Library Archives, Biddeford, Maine.
51. Spigel, *Welcome to the Dream House*, 57.
52. Segrave, *Drive-In Theaters*, 42.
53. Saco Motor-In Theater Advertisement, *Biddeford Saco Journal*, 1954, McArthur Library Archives, Biddeford, Maine.
54. Colauto, *Naked! Screaming! Terror!*, 42–52.
55. "Two Ton Tony's" real name was Domenicio Antionio Galento. He was an American heavyweight weighing 233 at the time of the fight. Joe Lewis won the fight in the fourth round, after two minutes and twenty-nine seconds. Motor-In Theatre Advertisement, July 25, 1939. *Biddeford Daily Journal*, McArthur Library Archives, Biddeford, Maine.
56. Segrave, *Drive-In Theaters*, 58.
57. Everett and McKeon, *Cinema Under the Stars*, 49.

58. Segrave, *Drive-In Theaters*, 59.
59. Ibid., 45.
60. Ibid., 62.
61. Everett and McKeon, *Cinema Under the Stars*, 43.
62. Ibid.
63. The suburban landscape merged the indoor and outdoor spaces and created one domestic space. Children played outside on the lawns of their homes or at neighborhood playgrounds. Parents planted gardens and took their families on picnics in local parks. The suburbs used scenes of nature within this new domestic space, just as the drive-in, set within a more rural landscape with trees and shrubbery, also became part of the domestic landscape. Spigel, *Make Room for TV*, 100.
64. By the 1950s, with the assistance of the American International Pictures, drive-ins achieved some financial stability and success, as they finally gained access to films on their first and second runs, no longer waiting until the fourth, fifth or later runs. Some of the B studios were Columbia Pictures, Universal and United Artists. Rhodes, *A Drive-In Horror by Default*, 54.
65. Heffernan, "Inner-City Exhibition," 60.
66. Segrave, *Drive-In Theaters*, 105.
67. By 1897, the *Nation* magazine reported "every mile on Maine's coast line from Kittery to Mount Desert Island had some marks of a summer resort." Judd writes, "In the face of surging recreational interest, Maine's landscape offered a new commercial potential, distinct from traditional land uses." The Saco Drive-In fits within this narrative of changing landscape for recreation. The drive-in maintains the rural landscape with trees and greenery while offering a twentieth-century amusement. Judd, "Reshaping Maine's Landscape," 189.
68. Everett and McKeon, *Cinema Under the Stars*, 70.

SOURCES

Bailey, Beth L. *From Front Porch to Back Seat: Courtship in Twentieth Century America*. Baltimore, MD: Johns Hopkins University Press, 1989.

Bassett, T.D. Seymour. "Documenting Recreation and Tourism in New England." *American Archivist* 4 (1987): 559–69.

Bell, Shannon. "From Ticket Booth to Screen Tower: An Architectural Study of Drive-In Theaters in the Baltimore-Washington, D.C.-Richmond Corridor." *Perspectives in Vernacular Architecture* (2003): 215–27.

Cohen Morley, Mary. "Forgotten Audiences in the Passion Pits: Drive-In Theatres and Changing Spectator Practices in Post-War America." *Film History* 6, no. 4 (1994): 470–86.

Colauto, Ricky J. "'Naked! Screaming! Terror!" In *Horror at the Drive-In: Essays in Popular Americana*. Edited by Gary Don Rhodes. Jefferson, NC: McFarland & Company Inc., 2003.

Everett, Linda, and Elizabeth McKeon. *Cinema Under the Stars: America's Love Affair with Drive-In Movie Theaters*. Nashville, TN: Cumberland House Publishing, 1998.

Fairfield, Roy P. "The Old Orchard 'Set-Off.'" *New England Quarterly* 2 (1954): 227–42.

———. *Sands, Spindles, and Steeples: A History of Saco, Maine*. Portland, ME: House of Falmouth, 1956.

Giles, Dennis. "The Outdoor Economy: A Study of the Contemporary Drive-In." *Journal of the University of Film and Video Association* 35, no. 2 (1983): 66–76.

SOURCES

Gross, Andrew S. "Cars, Postcards, and Patriotism: Tourism and National Politics in the United States, 1893–1929." *Pacific Coast Philology* 1 (2005): 77–97.

Heffernan, Kevin. "Inner-City Exhibition and the Genre Film: Distributing *Night of the Living Dead*." *Cinema Journal* 3 (2002): 59–77.

Hummon, David M. "Tourist Worlds: Tourist Advertising, Ritual, and American Culture." *Sociological Quarterly* 2 (1988): 179–202.

Judd, Richard W. "Reshaping Maine's Landscape: Rural Culture, Tourism, and Conservation, 1890–1929." *Journal of Forest History* 4 (1988): 180–90.

Kramer, Eric R. "Who's Afraid of the Virgin Wolfman?" In *Horror at the Drive-In: Essays in Popular Americana*. Edited by Gary Don Rhodes. Jefferson, NC: McFarland & Company Inc., 2003.

Lee, Michael. "Ideology and Style in the Double Feature *I Married a Murderer from Outer Space* and *Curse of the Demon*." In *Horror at the Drive-In: Essays in Popular Americana*. Edited by Gary Don Rhodes. Jefferson, NC: McFarland & Company Inc., 2003.

Mitman, Gregg. "Hay Fever Holiday: Health, Leisure, and Place in Gilded-Age America." *Bulletin on the History of Medicine* 3 (2003): 600–35.

Phillips, Kendall R. *Projected Fears: Horror Films and American Culture*. Westport, CT: Praeger, 2005.

Rhodes, Gary D. "A Drive-In Horror by Default, or, the Premiere of the Hideous Sun Demon." In *Horror at the Drive-In: Essays in Popular Americana*. Edited by Gary Don Rhodes. Jefferson, NC: McFarland & Company Inc., 2003.

Scharff, Virginia. *Taking the Wheel: Women and the Coming of the Motor Age*. Albuquerque: University of New Mexico Press, 1992.

Segrave, Kerry. *Drive-In Theaters: A History from Their Inception in 1933*. Jefferson, NC: McFarland & Company Inc., 2006.

Spigel, Lynn. *Make Room for the TV: Television and the Family Ideal in Postwar America*. Chicago: University of Chicago Press, 1992.

———. *Welcome to the Dream House: Popular Media and Postwar Suburbs*. Durham, NC: Duke University Press, 2001.

Weiss, Thomas. "Tourism in America before World War II." *Journal of Economic History* 2 (2004): 289–327.

Willis, Ian. "Whither Heritage, the Experience of the Outdoor Movie Theatre." *Australian Quarterly* 6 (2009): 35–39.

Wright, Virginia M. *Route 1: Maine*. Rockport, ME: Down East, 2013.

INDEX

ABOUT THE AUTHOR

Courtesy of Michael Strout Photography.

Camille Smalley grew up in Bremerton, Washington, and always loved history. She remembers watching various programs on the History Channel with her dad, as well as reading his many books about wars and battles. However, even though she enjoyed history and English courses while in high school, she never considered a career in history until she was halfway through college. At age seventeen, she moved to Maine and enrolled at the University of New England as an athletic training major. Having always enjoyed sports and athletic medicine in high school, it seemed like a natural fit. Smalley also enjoyed her English and women's and gender studies courses at the university and decided to switch to an English major with a women's and gender studies minor. She began taking courses with talented English, history and gender studies professors at the University of New England, many of whom inspired her to work in a completely different field than she had originally planned: history.

After taking a "Museums and Public History" course with history professor Elizabeth A. DeWolfe in 2007 and working as a museum assistant at the Dyer Library and Saco Museum, she decided that working on exhibitions and research was the perfect pathway for her. After graduating from the University of New England in 2008, Smalley was promoted at the Dyer Library and Saco Museum to the position of program and education manager. In 2010, she graduated from the University of Southern Maine with her master's in American and New England studies. Currently, she works at the Dyer Library and Saco Museum in Saco, Maine, as the collections and research manager, where she enjoys curating exhibitions, assisting with grant writing and researching artifacts. Along with Justin Chenette, Smalley assisted in founding the Saco Bay Center for Civic Engagement and serves as its executive vice-president. This nonprofit worked steadily to support the Saco Drive-In during its quest for a digital projector in 2013.

In her spare time, Smalley loves to read outside on a blanket, cook, bake, dance and go for long walks along Portland's Eastern Promenade. She currently lives in Portland, Maine, with her large black Maine coon cat named Wally.